DARK WOODS

Cults, Crime, and the Paranormal in the Freetown State Forest, Massachusetts

by Christopher Balzano

4880 Lower Valley Road, Atglen, Pennsylvania 19310

Published by Schiffer Publishing Ltd.
4880 Lower Valley Road
Atglen, PA 19310
Phone: (610) 593-1777; Fax: (610) 593-2002
E-mail: Info@schifferbooks.com

For the largest selection of fine reference books on this and
related subjects, please visit our web site at www.schifferbooks.
com. We are always looking for people to write books on new and
related subjects. If you have an idea for a book please contact us
at the above address.

This book may be purchased from the publisher.
Include $3.95 for shipping.
Please try your bookstore first.

You may write for a free catalog.

In Europe, Schiffer books are distributed by
Bushwood Books
6 Marksbury Ave.
Kew Gardens
Surrey TW9 4JF England
Phone: 44 (0) 20 8392-8585; Fax: 44 (0) 20 8392-9876
E-mail: info@bushwoodbooks.co.uk
Website: www.bushwoodbooks.co.uk
Free postage in the U.K., Europe; air mail at cost.

Cover photo by Justin Mycofsky
Copyright © 2008 by Christopher Balzano
Library of Congress Control Number: 2007933818

Designed by "Sue"
Type set in Stereofidelic /NewBskvll BT

ISBN: 978-0-7643-2799-5
Printed in China

DEDICATION

To my son, Devin, who has
taught me to look through the
eyes of innocence.

ACKNOWLEDGEMENTS

There are many people who contribute to the telling of the history of the town. I would like to first thank the people who allowed me to tell their stories. Their experiences are the backbone of this book. I would also like to thank the Freetown Historical Commission and the Freetown Historical Society for sharing their information and inviting me in. Special thanks go to Jeff Belanger and Tom D'Agostino for their encouragement and guidance. I am grateful for the help of Tim Weisberg, Matt Moniz, and Matt Costa from Spooky Southcoast for thinking people want to hear what I have to say, and to Loren Coleman, Christopher Pittman, and Aaron Cadieux for paving the way and giving me inspiration. I would like to acknowledge Sabina Besic for forcing me to keep going and Dave Turkalo for asking the question. My family has been crucial in getting me to this point, and I would like to say thank you to my mother and father. Jenna McFarland was the first to jump on the wagon and get Massachusetts Paranormal Crossroads going, and she was always ready to go out and investigate with me. This book is a result of the hard work and time of Alan Alves. Thank you for letting me listen and for the pages and pages and pages of history. Most of all, I would like to thank my wife, Jill. This book took many hours, and tanks of gas, and through it all, she remained my foundation, firmly on the ground, and my inspiration to reach higher. Thank you for thinking this thing could get done.

CONTENTS

INTRODUCTION

THE CURSED LAND

A statue dedicated to the CCC work-
ers who helped develop and maintain
the forest in its early years.

Do curses exist or are they the product of su-
perstition and retrospect? Why does the evil
in the world seem to find the same ground time
and time again? Why does the same land become
the stage for tragedy played out over time, taking different forms and affecting different people
from varied walks of life over centuries?

Can a place be born bad?

None of these questions were on my mind
when I first heard about Freetown, Massachusetts,
in the fall of 2003. I had been collecting ghost
stories and investigating hauntings for ten years

by that time, but I had never had to deal with some of the larger issues I found hiding in the forest of the southeastern part of my state. Many times there was a reason for a haunting I was reporting, and most times the reason became the story, but most were just odd voices heard in the night and things moving without living human hands. I never thought about evil, or curses or negative energy, and in many ways, I was unprepared for the world I was about to enter.

Then my boss asked me one day if I had ever heard any stories about Freetown. I had to be shown where it was on a map, and after doing some quick research, I decided it might be worth looking into. There were no written reports, and at that time, no collected rumors on the internet. A few quick ghost stories later I had the word out on my website and did not think much more of it. Much of what paranormal researchers do is like fishing in dark murky waters, and once my net was cast, the fish quickly found me.

Over the next three years, I found myself making the hour and a half drive out to the small rural community with half a foot in Rhode Island. It was not just the ghosts who were making themselves known in the town. I started to collect stories about Satanic cults, monsters, a triangle of mystery, and serial killers. It did not take me long to realize there was something about this place, some magnetism, acting as a beacon for misery.

I started to become a believer in curses.

Paranormal Investigating 101. Some people may see balls of light move across the room before rising to the ceiling and disappearing through the wall. Some people see a full-figured ghost standing over them at night or sitting on their chest sucking their air away. Others see heads without bodies, or hear disembodied voices calling their names or retelling conversations that happened decades ago. There have been reports of smelling flowers or garbage when a ghost is present. Depending on the haunting, someone can experience any number of dozens of symptoms, varying in degrees of intensity and frequency. There is, however, a common element to almost all paranormal experiences.

People *feel* ghosts.

Even if they do not smell them or hear them or see them, witnesses to the paranormal report *feeling* the spirit. Often times, an odd feeling is the only way to tell something is there. Your stomach jumps just a bit, or you feel nausea or suddenly full. The hairs go up on your arms and the back of your neck. The temperature may drop—but the feeling is more than that. You are not alone in the room. Something is watching you. The lights are on and no one is there, but you know better. You feel something is wrong.

As thinking, dreaming humans, we have overactive imaginations so we dismiss what our gut tells us. "It's just my imagination. I'm imagining things." If the haunting does not intensify, the experience ends there and we move on with our day. Countless hauntings go unnoticed and unreported because there is nothing more than a feeling. A sensation cannot be proven or documented and can be rationalized too easily. If you *see* something, it sticks. If you *hear* something, you can make yourself completely silent and try to hear it again. An investigator can snap a picture or record a voice with the right equipment. An emotional response, that sense of dread or uneasiness, cannot be captured, so the moment is left behind.

The odd thing is, our feelings are our most powerful sense. We feel with more passion than we smell, and usually we allow it to be good enough to prove something exists. Try and take a picture of love or hear hate. You can see the emotion in two people holding each other or the clenched fists of two people ready to fight. Think about the moment right before people jump and yell, "Surprise!" at a birthday party. Walk into a room where two people have just had a passionate argument. The sense of anticipation or anxiety creates electricity you can *feel*.

There is a link between energy and the paranormal that moves far beyond the hairs on the back of your neck. In the study of the paranormal, an investigator comes across this connection regularly. The most common haunting involves what investigators call a psychic recording. An event quickly gives off a massive amount of energy, imprinting the event in its environment. The right situation, whether it is another emotional trigger or the weather or the right person to perceive it, then triggers this energy and replays the event, like listening to the same song over and over again on the radio. An observer might hear footsteps the same time every night or see the image of a woman in old-fashioned clothes walk down the hallway and disappear without responding to being called or noticing her surroundings.

The most recognizable word in the study or the paranormal, even to those not familiar with it, is *poltergeist*. These tricky ghosts are thought to not be ghosts at all, but the result of telekinetic energy focused and released for a specific purpose. Almost all cases of true poltergeist activity involve a child during a specific stage of development, usually early childhood, puberty or post-pubescence. The child, more often than not a female, has often suffered some type of abuse, and while the poltergeist affects the entire household, violent attacks usually are levied against the victimizer or some archetypal aspect of the victimizer.

Demonologist say negative energy attracts demons to a certain area like vultures. They feed off this energy and in turn manipulate their environment to change the existing energy, creating a hell on Earth. This surrounds the victim with feelings of loneliness or helplessness, and this, in combination with a constant psychological and physical assault, prepares them for possession. After an exorcism, participants report the heaviness in the air lifts and the environment feels different. This is one of the signs that the ritual has worked.

Paranormal investigators and ghost hunters base their activities on energy. They use infrared cameras and nightglow goggles, believing the spirit will read a different temperature than the room. They measure radiation and electromagnetic waves in an area, and changes mean the presence of the paranormal. Photographs of balls of energy known as orbs constitute proof of a ghost. EVPs, or electronic voice phenomena, is the residue of a ghost caught electronically on tape. This is one of the reasons digital recorders pick up more EVPs than normal analogue. Scientists can dispute the validity of these approaches and the evidence gathered, but the antidotal evidence is overwhelming. People do experience ghosts and the temperature drops. Odd EMF readings are often found where hauntings have been reported.

Until now, there has always been a cause and effect relationship involving energy, mainly because of our need to find a reason for a haunting. We hate to think of ourselves as spirits not at peace, roaming the world of the living instead of finding salvation in heaven. We search for the roots of the haunting and gather historical evidence that might offer clues. A ghost might be someone who was killed and has unfinished business. A house was built on an ancient Indian burial ground or on the site of a murder. Haunted asylums or hospitals experience sightings because of the horrific conditions of the patients. A demon enters an environment because of a heinous sin committed.

These causes might explain some paranormal activity, but what if the trigger to the hauntings, what if the tragedy that set everything in motion, is the result of negative energy already in existence in the area? What if the murderer was compelled to kill, not by passion or revenge, but by some unseen force found naturally in the house? What if the heinous event that led to the possession happened for the same reason?

Places with high levels of paranormal activity also have a disproportionate amount of criminal activity and a higher level of mental health issues. This connection gets overlooked because very different people examine very different end results. A psychologist or a detective is not likely to think like a paranormal investigator.

Areas can be tainted. Cryptozoologists and people who study UFOs have a saying: If you see a Bigfoot, chances are someone has seen a UFO in the same area. There seems to be some type of energy attracting both of these paranormal creatures to the same place, and while it can be argued that two different observers can classify the same experiences as an alien or a Bigfoot, the list of unexplained occurrences in specific places extends well beyond a difference in frame of reference.

Catholic churches around the world, especially in Ireland and other part of Britain, are built on the same plots of land as more ancient places of worship. While part of this is attributed to the conversion of conquered cultures, one has to ask if there is a pull to the spot from two different religions.

Freetown lies at the crossroads of this type of energy. It is hard to say if the land was always cursed or whether the tragedy played out over time has just fed itself, but compare the town to others like it across the country and you will start to see the differences. Freetown could be any town, but as you look deeper, as you start to listen to the whispers, history begins to poke its head out.

The heart of the town is the state forest. Everything begins with what walks among the trees there and most of the criminal investigations have their starting or ending points somewhere off the dirt bike paths that cut through the woods. The energy braches out, though. There are haunted schools and buildings within the town lines, but Freetown is a town that has evolved through the years. The original borders have been cut and reassigned and made into other towns and cities that owe their history to the original tract settled in 1657. No complete story can be told without looking at these places as well.

Most of what makes up this book comes from the people who experienced it, but much of it also is the child of legend and urban legend. Over three hundred and fifty years those lines get blurred, and looking at official documents can never tell the full story. Some of the stories come from news reports about true crime, but police reports only tell us the facts and leave out the emotion.

I recently spoke at a meeting of the Freetown Historical Commission who invited me after hearing I was writing a book on ghosts of their town. They thought it was odd and had never really heard the stories before, but ghost story after ghost story met with nods and uncomfortable laughter. More than a dozen had heard the legend of the Pukwudgie. The tales were all around them, and when the light of day was shed, they all had something to share.

Any story of a town is never the full story. In the past three years, I have met people who teach, inspire, and love. They are not the reason for the curse, but are rather branches caught in the storm. For them, the curse is in the background, soft music going unnoticed while the scene plays out. They do not ask why the darkness has visited their town, but instead do not realize there is a light to be seen. They go about their days, going to school and work and raising families, but do not see they share the land with something unexplained.

All of the stories in this book are true, or as true as any ghost story can be. They are the words of ordinary people retelling a snapshot of their lives. The true crime aspects are gathered from news reports, published material, and first-hand accounts. Confirming a rumor is like analyzing a dream: everyone has their version of the truth.

Whenever possible, I have inserted disclaimers of established fact and legend, but even the truth needs a translator. The names have been changed in most cases, but there has been no change on the impact of their experiences.

If curses exist, the people of Freetown know its results. There is no fog over the land or old witch in the forest (well, maybe one) shaking her finger at the generations that passed before her. Instead there is something unexplained and unexplored, turning with the town and coming to the surface every once in a while. Many come to Freetown, drawn by the state forest and its physical beauty. This is the story of those who cannot leave.

CHAPTER 1

FROM ONE KETTLE

In the summer of 2006, a longstanding tradition in the State Forest in Freetown, Massachusetts, was reborn. As gas prices soared around the country, people began dumping their cars in the forest. Most reported them stolen, knowing it would be weeks or months before their cars were found. It was a popular activity during the gas crisis of the 1970s and came back during the hard times in the late 1980s and 1990s when it was common to set your car on fire before you abandoned it. With over five thousand acres of land to hide in and limited law enforcement and park rangers to patrol, the forest was a perfect hiding place.

The cars were a nuisance, but represented the only connection to the dark past the forest had become infamous for. Today, the landscape bears little resemblance to the woods of just twenty years ago. The trees and natural features are the same, but the air is different. Families have started coming back, most of whom know little if anything of the history that earned the area its nickname: the dumping ground of Southeastern Massachusetts. The name extends beyond the cars and waste that have made the woods their home. The past two decades have been spent rebuilding a relationship with the town, with cleaning the graffiti off the rocks and trees, and with convincing the public the paths are safe. On the surface, it is now more about family fun and nature walks and less about ghosts, monsters, and dead bodies.

The forest, which technically lies in both Fall River and Freetown, has undergone a facelift and public relations overhaul. Although numbers are hard to come by because of the numerous entrances, the paths fill with 15,000 people a year, most in the summer months. They enjoy the newly-lined wading pool and picnic tables, or bike the miles of trials snaking through the trees. It is mostly local families who come after work to enjoy the peaceful atmosphere, but during the weekend the license plates read like a map of New England: New Hampshire, Connecticut, Rhode Island.

Freetown is like many small towns in New England. Finding it on a map usually means looking for its larger, more known neighbors and then carefully weeding through the print to find the small letters. It is the kind of town you passed through the edge of getting somewhere else or see on a sign on the highway and never give a second thought to. One of its two public libraries is hidden inside what looks like a quaint colonial bungalow, and the books are placed haphazardly, somewhat following the dewy decimal system. In many ways, the town revolves around the forest.

Mentioning Freetown to a resident of eastern Massachusetts is a bit different. They might not be able to find it on a map, but they remember it somehow. They think something happened there once. They know the name. The events that unfolded there, more often than not remembered by their details and not the names involved, cover the past thirty years like small stepping stones stretching out over decades.

The town was not a place people stayed. The Wampanoag tribe, the first inhabitants of the town, used the land only seasonally, and never created lasting settlements there. It was purchased by the English as an investment, a strategic location with waterfront and resources. As the towns around it grew, there seemed to always be something keeping Freetown back.

History is written in black and white, pushing aside anything unexplained and offering the clearest definitions and reasons leading from point A to point B. Events are carried on the backs of real people, often flawed and always very human. Freetown stands as a symbol of the history of the area, never really known, but always at its forefront. A former law enforcement office from the town observed this for decades while on the force. "Whatever weird things happen, they seem to happen here first. We're always on the cutting edge of the odd." That is the legacy of the town. They have acted as a magnet for the unexplained for centuries, maybe longer.

The troubles with Freetown, and any possible curse there, date back to long before the English ever arrived. Aaron Cadieux, a local filmmaker from a neighboring town, explored the era in his film, *The First Patriot*. The movie is a chronicle of

King Philip's War and offers insight into relations between the Native Americans and the settlers from the landing of the Mayflower until the end of the bloody conflict. In his extensive research, he has interviewed historians, academics, and members of the different tribes in the area. He has discovered everything was not right in America before the English arrived.

"The existence of intertribal friction before the English arrived was something [the British] could exploit at the outbreak of war. They would rather side with the English than a tribe they might have had a feud with. They couldn't set aside their differences and unite as one against a common enemy." Instead, the different tribes used their relationships with the colonists as a bargaining chip with their own people and a way to intimidate their rivals. Those who did not work to form strong binds with the new strangers soon found themselves loosing power in their own region.

The story of the town starts several decades before it was bought by the British. Between 1614 and 1620, disease spread through the people, reducing the Wampanoag numbers from 12,000 to 2,000 and greatly reducing their military and political power. The Narragansett were almost untouched by the plagues, and by the time the English began to settle in large numbers, their strength dwarfed their rivals.

The Spanish had already conquered the tribes of Central and South America, but the English considered themselves more civil. The Native Americans heard rumors of the atrocities the Spanish had committed in their quest for land, and the few minor battles between them and the English taught them what the Europeans were capable of. The English could kill large numbers of people quickly and showed little interest for the type of fighting they had become used to.

The English were gaining power and spreading their beliefs. Cadieux evaluated the causes of conflict between the new neighbors in Massachusetts. He believes the heart of the conflict comes from the settlers.

"The Puritans came over here and, based on their beliefs and lifestyle, tried to force their ways upon the Native Americans." While they were successful at converting some Native Americans and establishing Christian towns, their new laws and pushing their weight around pushed the other Native Americans to the brink of war."

Massasoit, the Wampanoag sachem, knew the only way to survive the English and the growing number of Native enemies all around him was to join Plymouth Colony. It was a one-sided union, as Massasoit was forced to swear allegiance to Britain and the king and received nothing but protection in return. A new form of conquering was developing. The English would offer the Wampanoag products they had never seen before on credit with land as collateral. The English would then limit trade and trapping rights, and when the Natives could not repay their debt, the English would take over the land.

Although it was not completely to his advantage, Massasoit knew that agreeing to the bad land deals was the only way for his people to survive, so he continued to ally himself with the English and allow land to be sold.

Freetown is rumored to have been born this way. Massasoit's son Wamsutta, who was also known as Alexander, took control after his death.

He was bound to repay his father's debt, including a large drinking tab at a tavern owned by John Barnes. In 1659, with his hands tied, Alexander agreed to the Freeman's Purchase. For his father's bill being cleared, some clothes, and alcohol, the English received almost thirty square miles of land on the Assonet River. One of the witnesses who is reported to have encouraged Alexander, was a Wampanoag named John Sassamon who would later ignite war between the two parties.

Land was only one problem for the Wampanoag. The English saw it as their duty to preach the word of God to the people. Those who converted had special privileges in court and business dealings. They were treated differently, and pressure was applied to the leaders from all the tribes. English laws limited the ownership of goods and hunting rights for Non-Christian Natives and trade was more common between Christians. More Native Americans converted, probably more out of a sense of survival than a genuine change of religious belief, and as more became what was called Praying Indians, the more sachems struggled to maintain their strength.

The Freetown Purchase was to be the last major land deal between the Wampanoags and Plymouth. In 1662, Alexander was called to appear before the court in Plymouth, and he and his followers were taken by gunpoint up the coast. At some point, Alexander became sick and asked to return home. He died before reaching his tribe. His wife, Wetamoe, the Queen of the Pocasset Indians, and his brother, Metacom, or Philip, believed he had been poisoned by the English. This anger and mistrust followed the two of them through the next decade as Philip took over control of the tribe and Wampanoags continued to find Christ.

Rival sachems began launching accusations against Philip, claiming he was trying to start a war with the British. Each time, he was hauled into court and cleared of the charge, but he was quickly losing Plymouth's trust. In 1671, he was hauled in again because several of his followers had showed their guns to the English. To avoid conflict, Philip confessed they might be part of a plot to attack the English. The weapons were taken away, but five months later, he was brought back and accused of harboring criminals against the English.

Meanwhile, John Sassamon, the witness of the Freetown Purchase, was gaining more power. Threatened by the strength of the other Wampanoags, he too accused Philip of planning to revolt against the English. A month later he was reported missing, and eventually his body was discovered under the ice. The English, believing him murdered, assumed it was Philip and his followers. Three Wampanoags, Tobias, Wampapaquan, and Mattashunannamp were found guilty and executed. It proved to be the best example of the power of Praying Indians over the Wampanoag and the final straw that led to war.

As all of the events of the past few decades— the murder of his brother, the followers leaving by the dozens, and the killing of men found guilty with no evidence—swirled about him, the paranormal stepped in. In an often overlooked nod to the unknown, a total lunar eclipse occurred. The Native Americans in the area saw this as a sign of war and Philip used this to fuel their desire for change. Metamoe agreed with her brother-in-law and offered her troops as well. Swansea was attacked and King Philip's war began.

Over the next eighteen months, the area, including Freetown, became the battle scene of some of the most heinous fighting the continent has ever witnessed. Aaron Cadieux has spent years collecting stories about the war, especially the viciousness of the fighting and the devastation of the end results. "The violence was, per capita, the bloodiest in American history, with a death rate higher than the Civil War. There were towns in Massachusetts that were not resettled until seventy years after the war because their economic conditions were so bad."

Instead of battles where the two forces faced each other across a field and fought to the death, both sides adopted a hit and run approach to warfare. Raid after raid was conducted against both sides, resulting in the slaughter of soldiers, but also women and innocent children. Traditional enemies joined together, but brothers and fathers also chose different sides. There was no moral compass to the fighting, fueling rumors later that the people seemed possessed by the devil.

One of the most appalling moments of the war came to be known as the Great Swamp Massacre. Fearing the Narragansett would join the Wampanoags, the English decided to launch a massive preemptive strike with 1,000 men against them in the town of South Kingston, Rhode Island. Governor Winslow of Massachusetts led the attack himself, and in December of 1675, 600 Native Americans were killed, mostly women and children living in wigwams in the middle of the swamp. The causalities to the Narragansett warriors, protected by the walls of a garrison, were minimal.

Cadieux has discovered even more tragedies in his research. At Turner Falls in Greenfield, Massachusetts, four innocent people, two of them children, were hiding from the English when they were discovered, interrogated, and decapitated. The English captain, Samuel Mosley, employing Dutch pirates he had captured off the coast, used dogs to track the Native Americans and once allowed them to devour an innocent woman he had questioned.

In the wake of the war, the landscape of New England changed greatly. The English abandoned a third of their towns, including Freetown. Ten percent of the people involved in the war, including innocents, were wounded or killed. The Wampanoags, already depleted by the plagues and converts, reduced their numbers by forty percent.

Many see this as the beginning of the curse on Freetown. The bloodshed and death (often of children and noncombatants) and betrayal felt could produce enough negative energy to punch a hole into another dimension or imprint themselves in the air and replaying themselves over like a skipping record. Perhaps the souls of all those lost are trapped on earth trying to find a reason for their deaths. Maybe the negative intentions on both sides could become an actual curse left behind to fall on future generations.

It would seem all of these are possible truths in the town, but the curse might go further back. Why were the Wampanoags so devastated by the plagues and disease while their neighbors seemed immune? Why were the English in the area, so determined to escape the folly of their Spanish counterparts, so quick to become what they hated and slaughter innocent people? Like many crimes committed in Freetown, the violence during that time is disproportionate to the situation, and while battles occurred in most parts of central New England, the worst of the war crimes happened in southeastern Massachusetts.

Did the war cause the curse or was the war itself a result of some older, dark force at work years before the Europeans arrived?

Many accounts of King Philip's War talk about the effects in an abstract way. Both sides lost a part of their souls, but in a very concrete way, the English won. They eventually reopened their settlements in southeastern Massachusetts, including the parcel of land they had originally called Freeman's Town.

Following the development of the town and surrounding area is much like trying to follow a ping pong ball being slapped across a table. It would seem it was expanded in the late 1670s with the Pocasset Purchase. Due to their distance from Plymouth Colony, land seemed to flow more freely and become named and renamed with each owner. The original founders adopted the motto, "From one small kettle," and it proved to be an accurate description of a town part of, or claimed ownership of, almost every town surrounding it.

The town was officially established in 1683. In 1747, part of the Rhode Island town of Tiverton was annexed and became part of Freetown. In 1803, Fall River broke off and established itself as a separate city, becoming more prosperous than Freetown, if not more infamous, and suffering its own tragedies over the years. In 1815, Fairhaven, Massachusetts, annexed part of Freetown, establishing what is now still roughly their modern border. The curse of Freetown, however, has always found a way to surface in the area, whether the land is recognized as Fall River or Assonet or East Freetown.

During this time, Freetown seemed a step behind in its ability to adapt and grow. During the American Revolution, it sided with the English and was a favorite target of the Americans. Taunton, Massachusetts, was a hotbed of rebel activity, and the Colonel Thomas Gilbert of Freetown was called upon to defeat them, although he was never successful. After that, rebels would attack Freetown at will. The town divided its loyalties until the last Tory was forced out late in 1776. In 1778, 150 British troops, under the leadership of Major John Ayre, traveled up the Taunton River to recapture the area. The Battle of Freetown ensued, with almost no loss of life and no land changing hands. Even in war, Freetown could not distinguish itself.

There was another tragedy that happened on Freetown's soil that might explain the negative energy. While no longer written in history books and now living more in the realm of legend, it might be the darkest days of the town.

While reading up on the history of Freetown, former police detective Alan Alves took a book out of the library. He cannot remember the exact title, but he remembers reading a section about Pre-Civil War New England and the abolishment of slavery in the northern states. He claims to have read a passage telling of several slave owners taking their slaves into the forest, killing them, and burying them all in an unmarked mass grave. The story disturbed him enough to show his wife, who confirms his story. He returned the book, but tried to take it out again after getting into an argument with someone over the facts. The book was taken out, and over the next few months he tried to reserve a copy or find it in another library. He never saw it again. Very soon after the incident, a new edition of the title came out. The section on the killings was not part of the new printing.

None of the details of the story can be confirmed, but doubt still lingers. Too much has happened in Freetown to disregard such a tale, and Alves swears to the existences of the chapter. It might account for some of the unexplained happenings in the forest, although no sightings involving African Americans has ever been reported.

In 1934, the forest, officially the Freetown-Fall River State Forest, was established. Its development was left in the hands of the CCC, or the Civilian Conservation Corp. Today, a statue stands as a testament to their work in the forest. They worked to develop roads and trails, and the grounds actually became a training camp for the program nationwide. Today, some of their structures can still be seen, including two massive chimneys that jump out of the woods.

Around the same time, a treaty was signed giving the Wampanoags a section of the land in the forest as a reservation. The reservation was repayment for land taken to establish the Fall River watersheds. Today, it is only a part time home for them again, used primarily for annual ceremonies and important meetings. The relationship between the Wampanoags and the people who visited the forest has been strained at times, but there has never really been any trouble between the two. To the Native Americans who go to the

One of the old fireplaces in ruin within the forest.

reservation, the land is sacred, but some have come out and said they feel something dark in the forest.

Some feel the curse on the paths traversing the woods. Most acknowledge a heavy presence of spirits in the forest, even if they feel the ghosts might be positive and trying to pass on secrets of the past. Others just know things feel different there. Barry, a local teen, tries to stay away from the forest at night, even when his friends want to go. "Sometimes if you're out in the forest at night, you get a real eerie feeling. Just a vibe. You don't want to be there. You just want to turn around and get out."

Over the next seventy years, the town and the forest have suffered too many tragedies to be dismissed as coincidence. They are the adopted home to criminals from the worst section of the worst cities neighboring them. The horrors seem to come like heartbeats, surfacing every few years and acting as a harbinger for things happening across the country. In recent days, park rangers and fire officials have worked hard to change the reputation of the forest, but all of the new planting and rock cleanings cannot fully change the picture people have in their heads about Freetown. Families are more likely to come today, but they remember the names and the whispers. The forest is maintained and protected by several different agencies and friends groups, and their efforts have made the woods more appealing to out-of-towners, but sometimes hardship dies hard and the fingerprints of misfortune are slow to fade.

Most places have some history of ghosts or legends of monsters, and all places have crimes that confuse the community. In Freetown, these things happen at a quicker pace and make more headlines. Law enforcement states this is due to its proximity to several large cities, and the area becomes a safe getaway for crimes born somewhere else, but they do come. There are other places to hide one's sins, but in Freetown, sin might beget sin and attract others to come and celebrate a safe haven and join a club started before the English arrived and has no real end in sight.

CHAPTER 2

THE BRIDGEWATER TRIANGLE: AN APEX IN CONTEXT

The southeastern section of Massachusetts has always been known as a bit odd. It is the foundation of English settlement and the heart of the state's Native American culture, but it often gets overlooked in the overall history of New England. It is the genesis of our modern culture, however. Tales have been passed down from tribal fires to campfires since before there were books to write them down in. The Native Americans in the area feared what might lurk in the swamps there, and as more and more settlers found their way to the rivers and forests and the towns began to gather more people, legend became experience.

The towns that became the backbone of Massachusetts have never been able to prosper, while the surrounding areas have. The cities to the south in Rhode Island, such as Providence and Newport, flourished. Boston and Cape Cod are more important to the outsider and account for the modern tourism dollars Massachusetts earns. Even the towns to the west such as Springfield and Worcester are more likely to earn a dot on a map than New Bedford or Fall River.

Why has this area been left behind by history and ignored by the present? The answer might lie in a paranormal trend that has gained recent attention from all types of investigators of the unknown. The supernatural can be found in any town, and a good investigator can make camp in an unfamiliar place and find evidence, but some places have so many incidents that remain unexplained, they somehow seem to shout out to be noticed.

The sheer number of experiences in South-eastern Massachusetts finally gained national attention with the publication of Loren Coleman's 1983 book, *Mysterious America*. Coleman, considered by most people in the field to be the public face of modern cryptozoology, investigated odd cases in Massachusetts during the seventies and early eighties. He began to see trends contained in the towns of Bridgewater, East Bridgewater, and West Bridgewater, forming a natural triangle. He expanded it to include other locations as he discovered new cases, until it took the form he included in his book. He christened the area the Bridgewater Triangle and the name stuck. Two corners of his triangle are the towns of Abington and Rehoboth. The third is Freetown. Contained in this 200 square-mile area are the towns of Brockton, Raynham, Taunton, Bridgewater, Mansfield, Norton, and Easton. The Triangle touches two different counties, Bristol and Plymouth.

To paranormal investigators in the area, the Triangle is a goldmine. Standing on a street corner is likely to result in being told some story of the unexplained. The area is known for heightened reports of monsters and odd animals, and is a hotbed of UFO activity. Much of this can be explained away by people who do not believe in the supernatural, but there are other signs that the area might be a magnet for negative activity.

Within the borders of the Triangle, anything seems possible. There have been reports of Bigfoot and giant thunderbirds. One report even has a Bigfoot-like monster picking up the back of a police cruiser. Some have seen snakes larger than anacondas or beasts describes as werewolves. UFO sightings happen there on a regular basis, some reported by local authorities. Air Force One even reported seeing something it could not explain in the skies above.

Documentary filmmaker Aaron Cadieux is the head of the independent film company Big Operations Productions. He spends most of his time working on local football games and producing short films about the area, including *A Time to Reflect: The History of Whalom Park*, about a local amusement park. He is not a paranormal investigator and considers himself a skeptic about the stories people tell about his area of the state. In 2003, however, he was intrigued enough by the stories his friends were telling to look more closely at them. He did more research on the internet, and one phrase kept coming up.

"I kept hearing about the Bridgewater Triangle. It was all places I had heard, in towns that I knew. I'd hear a story and say, 'Rehoboth is right near me,' or, 'I spend time in Bridgewater.' I knew I wanted to make a film about it because it had not been done before."

Inside the Bridgewater Triangle was produced and released in 2003, and quickly became a cult classic among the paranormal community. In it, Cadieux documents the unusual happenings in several of the towns included in the Triangle, including an investigation conducted by the Cape and Islands Paranormal Research Society. Of all of his research, he found the material about Freetown the most upsetting. He focused on the cult activity in the forest, interviewing some of the key people involved in the investigations and reviewing the evidence they had collected himself.

"It was by far the most disturbing. There are many things I showed that I'm skeptical about, but this was real. This really happened and it's all documented." Although he is not a full believer in many of the paranormal aspects of the Triangle, he concedes there are too many stories and too much back story in the area to overlook.

Freetown's place within the Triangle might be more important than just being one of the corners. Traditionally, the heart of the Bridgewater Triangle is a wet, wooded area known as the Hockomock Swamp. It is a natural choice. It is located in the middle of Coleman's defined lines and represents the stories he had collected. It is a prime spot to look for animals off the maps because so much of it remains undeveloped.

When he originally published *Mysterious America,* Coleman intended his lines to be the template for future investigators to evaluate and build upon. This included different types of cases and the inclusion of more geographical locations. There are many aspects Coleman chose not to include in his original equation, and when these are examined and the Triangle stretched out, Freetown takes it place not as an apex, but as the heart.

First, there is a limit to the cases Coleman included in his work. In a recent interview, he indicated he does not focus on ghosts. This caused him to leave out one of the most important aspects of Southeastern Massachusetts. While the entire state boasts a high number of phantoms, by far this area has more reports of activity than anywhere else. In recent days, investigators have added hauntings to the list he started, and only now are they starting to see a possible connection between Coleman's reports and theirs.

Coleman also focused on things that could be seen or measured because of his training and focus. The Bridgewater Triangle, however, does not just boast haunted buildings and Bigfoot. There is also a negative energy there that cannot be measured or quantified, but whose effects are felt throughout the area. Massachusetts is notorious for recycling old buildings. As one of the havens for the sick during the heyday of tuberculosis, the state built several sanitariums for rich patron throughout the country. There was a very low success rate in dealing with the disease, but these hospitals were believed to minimize the pain felt by the patients. Many died, but when the outbreaks slowed down, the structures were often changed to accommodate state agencies. This same history repeats itself for other traditional hospitals, prisons, and mental health facilities in the state.

The result is a wealth of old abandoned buildings and juvenile criminal treatment facilities in Bristol and Plymouth County. These towns seem to house more hospitals for the treatment of mental disorders than any others surrounding them. Many of these facilities have seen different types of sadness and horror for generations, giving them plenty of time to have spirits stay behind or to have negative energy build up.

While these hospitals treat patients (many of them youth), from across the state, it would seem throughout their history, they have attracted the disturbed. There is also a heightened rate of unusual and cult-related crime. While Boston might get the attention of the national media, it is in Plymouth and Bristol County where reports of serial killers and famous murders take place.

Loren Coleman did not make the connection between mental health and the paranormal in his original writings on the Triangle. He has, however, touched upon this relationship in other works and written extensively on the connection between crime in certain areas and events like suicide clusters and their connection to the media. There is heightened crime, suicide, and mental disorder rarely linked to the paranormal and the causal effect of these two seemingly independent issues is not often examined.

The lines of the Triangle are defined by man-made town borders. The paranormal does not know these limits and does not hesitate to walk over them. In fact, most towns do not maintain their boundaries over the years. This is even more pronounced when you look at the history of Freetown. This means the lines might extend even beyond Massachusetts into several towns in Rhode Island suffering from the same symptoms as any within the traditional boundaries.

When these other cities are thrown into the mix, and all the other confines of Coleman's original map are factored in, the physical and conceptual heart of the Triangle begins to lean towards Freetown. The Hockomock Swamp might be the more famous of the two, but the Freetown State Forest is the true symbol of the evil living there, a force that continues to draw in more negative energy regardless of what geometrical figure we apply to it.

The legend of the Bridgewater Triangle grows every year. Around Halloween, all of the local papers and the larger publications out of Boston scramble to fill their pages with tales from within the infamous boundaries Coleman investigated over two decades ago. The legend needs to evolve as well, and the evidence is there to be discovered if the explorer keeps an open mind. The Triangle will continue to attract the curious, but it might be the new questions yet to be asked that keep the spirit of the legends alive.

CHAPTER 3

NATIVE AMERICAN GHOSTS

One of the roads within the forest where
the ghost of a Native America was seen.

M any hauntings fall into the realm of legends in a land as old as Massachusetts, and current reports as well as old folktales fall into basic motifs seen for almost 400 years. This does not invalidate reports as being untrue or merely a symptom of misunderstanding or fear. There is that element to them. Rather, they help explain the possibilities of why these hauntings may be true.

The Freetown State Forest has its share of Native American ghosts. Most who experience them are sure of what they have seen and somehow feel touched. In the forest, the tradition of Indians in ghost stories gets twisted. People experience humans who are Native Americans and not the Native Americans as the cause of the haunting. For years, Native Americans have been the reason for a haunting. The idea of the ancient burial ground often comes up in reports of ghosts. The story is usually the same. Unexplained things happen in a location, most often poltergeist-like activity and odd dreams, and a deeper investigation reveals the house was built on an ancient Indian burial ground. The family is forced to leave the house or somehow expel the spirit or purify the land. This really means cleaning out the old to make room for the new.

The concept is scary, the first essential element to a good ghost story. It invades your house where you are supposed to feel safe. Also included in this motif are instances where artifacts are removed and continue to curse or haunt those who take them.

It is important to note the wording of the phrase used in this kind of report because it is always the same. Take the words, "ancient" and

"Indian." "Ancient" allows us to see Native Americans as old, outdated, and somehow mystic. The use of the word, "Indian" helps paint a picture of the classic images of the people. Never is the more politically correct term used. "Cemetery" is never used in place of "burial ground," creating a foreign feel that further serves to separate. This concept has been seen in movies for years. It is interesting to note the modern day version of this tale where the American house is built on a cemetery, like in the movie *Poltergeist*. The interesting aspect is there are very few, if any, tales of this type of haunting in folklore until after Native American culture influences European and American storytelling.

There are several stories of burial grounds covered over in the forest. No one can be sure of exactly where they are, but the tales abound. One would be naïve to think there are not Wampanoags cemeteries in the forest, especially with so many places considered scared and current Native Americans feeling connected there.

Another motif is the appearance of phantoms seen as lights or orbs. In Wampanoag legend there is the Tei-Pai-Wankas, which are said to be the spirits of people who have passed, most often the souls of people killed by Pukwudgies. These are seen in several places throughout the forest, including the Assonet Ledge, Profile Rock, and the Wampanoag Reservation. Although there have been physical attacks at these sites, the bulk of the reports seem to be focused more on keeping the grave memory of what happened there alive. Full-bodied spirits are sometimes seen looking lost or confused or reenacting the tragedy that happened. Voices or the sounds of some action are heard. Other times an unknown feeling over-whelms people. They sense they are unwelcome and should leave. People report feeling like they are being watched.

Given the area and nature of the original settlers of New England, relationships between the soci-eties were destined to create folklore and tales of spirits. Confusion, fear, and miscommunications laid the groundwork for hostility, and those hos-tilities flourished into traditions. Again, this ap-pears to validate the cynics who say paranormal activity is in the participant's mind. Some of these tales, especially those who follow established folk motifs, may very well have never happened, or originated in truth and then found themselves changed and manipulated by time.

There is little doubt some of the hauntings out there are little more than cultural propaganda, but there are other reasons for the activity report-ed and for the survival of the legends.

Native American religion might be the source for actual hauntings as well. Their connection to the spirits they saw made hauntings very much a real-ity in their lives and more then likely to be sensi-tive to paranormal elements. The existence of ghosts was an integral part of their religion, not in opposition to it. Whether they were endowed with certain powers after death cannot be said, but it would at least make them open if that sort of thing was possible. At the very least, their deep religious connection with nature would prompt them to come back to defend their land and seek revenge for promises broken.

In the Freetown State Forest, the Native American hauntings are concentrated in several areas, but there are other sightings throughout the forest.

The origin of these spirits is unknown, but the one disturbing aspect of the sighting is the random nature of the occurrence. The areas are well traveled and well known to people who frequent the forest, but for some reason, on this one day, the other side made itself known.

In the northwest section of the forest is a scenic route known as Breakneck Trail. The path is used for hiking, but is one of the most common trails used by horses. Juan often jogs the course because of its distance from the major attractions of the forest. He enjoys cutting across nearby Massasoit Trail and making his way to the railroad tracks before coming back up and returning to his car. He enjoys doing it alone, but remembers the day he had a pace runner in front of him.

"When I first saw him in front of me, I thought he was just another runner. I usually don't see people out here, so I noticed him right away. I remember thinking it was weird he didn't have any shoes on, but I know people that do that, so I brushed it off."

Juan says he watched the man without much interest until he was about halfway to the end of the trail. "I saw him start floating. He wasn't floating away or anything, he was just not touching the ground any more. His feet were moving like he was running, but he was a few inches off the ground." Juan stopped running as soon as he noticed the man's feet, but was surprised when the phantom runner stayed in the same place, even though his feet were still moving. After a few seconds he dissipated before Juan's eyes.

"I got the feeling I was supposed to see him. He stayed in my line of sight right up until he disappeared. I don't know why, but there was some reason I saw him."

Juan describes the man as a little over five feet tall and said he was wearing what looked like tan biker shorts and no shirt. His skin was well tanned, but his long dark hair and his lack of shoes made him feel the man was a Native American. Although he admits to having heard stories of ghosts in the woods before that day, he does not feel as if he imagined the spirit or it influenced his opinion as to the race of the ghost.

A similar experience was shared by Lisa, a long time resident who has spent hundreds of hours in the forest over the years. While walking her dog a few years ago off the parking lot on Slab Bridge Road, Lisa encountered what she believes was the spirit of a departed Wampanoag. It had snowed a few days before, and the majority of paths still had sections covered. Her dog had started down an unpaved road when it stopped and stared ahead, something Lisa says her high-strung dog never did. She approached her dog and noticed a man disappear around the turn in the road. She did not get a good look at the time and found no reason to be scared. The two of them kept on the path, but when they turned the corner, she saw the man again.

The ghost was maybe sixteen or seventeen and was wearing no clothes and no shoes, a fact that struck Lisa as odd because she was feeling the cold winter breeze with her coat and wool hat on. He was walking away from her, so she was not able to get a look at his face, but approximately three second later the man dissolved into nothingness. During the entire occurrence, he had a light blue aura around him and did not seem entirely there.

Most who come face to face with the spirits in the woods do not see a face at all. Even in the winter, the employees at the fire barn are on the lookout for the typical forest outbreaks, but some of the fire have no explanation and disappear as soon as they flare up.

These phantom fires are seen in every corner of the woods, usually deeper in the trees where the paths become not much more than compacted grass worn by travel. People see them at a distance and are drawn to them for reasons they cannot remember, although most are able to at least say part of it is curiosity. When they get close to them, the fires dissolve.

The characteristics of the fire itself is what disturbs the people. There is no heat emanating from them, and there is no sound of wood burning. There is no smell of smoke. The flames are normal at first glance, but almost all state there is a greenish-blue outline to them and the smoke never moves past the tint.

"I don't know why I thought it had something to do with Indians," remembers Lenny, now in his early forties. He witnessed the fires near the Fall River line in the summer of 1997 and was more amazed then scared by the event. "I just got a feeling I was seeing something from years ago, like before we [English settlers] got here. I've heard some people say they hear chanting or yelling when they see them, but not me. Maybe I was just thinking it was an Indian because of the stories I heard, but I got that feeling."

Lenny reports he saw three fires on the path in a triangle twenty yards ahead of him. He could not smell anything from them and remembers feeling no heat as he approached. The fires were several feet apart, allowing him to step between them. When he reached the middle, they all disappeared.

There can be a debate on the nature of ghosts. An examination of hauntings over thousands of years reveals the same ghosts making their presence known in different places with different names. A vampire appearing in Romania starts to mirror one found in Rhode Island. This lends credibility to people who firmly state the paranormal should be seen as fiction, the recycling of folk beliefs passed off as fact. Fact or fiction, Native Americans have played an important role in the paranormal history of this country. Examining haunted burial grounds and rivers, looking at the folklore passed down, debating the truth of these tales strengthens our identity as Americans and brings history back into our mind's eye.

CHAPTER 4

THE RESERVATION

Most of the Freetown State Forest is a maze, and tracking down haunted locations can be like trying to find a needle in a stack of needles. The area is often off the path and usually intimidating, even when the sun finds its way through the trees. It adds to the fear many feel just being inside the forest and only increases as you learn more of what has happened there.

The exception is the Wampanoag Reservation off High Street and Ledge Road. In a collage of mixed and matched puzzle pieces, it is the one constant, recognizable thing people agree on. Located right off the main road, someone spends more time walking around, marveling at the trees and high grass than stomping through the woods trying to find their way on the map. It is not just the location drawing people to the spot, though.

The reservation is the most peaceful place within the forest. There are manmade structures in the main area just off the road, but almost immediately after leaving them, you come to paths cutting into the forest. Most are no more than hints of a way to go, worn down by foot traffic and not machine, and crossroads lead to other crossroads. It would be easy to get lost jumping from one trail to the other, following the trees growing straight, with no hint of changing light and passing other trees slumping down, almost blocking the route in front of you. With its natural beauty and palpable positive energy, it might not be a bad place to get lost.

One of the haunted areas within the Reservation.

Keeping in line with the traditions of reservations throughout the country, it is its own place, part of the forest and the history there, but reserving its own identity and shunning the reputation of other spots in Freetown. For the most part, bad things do not happen there. Some have experienced negative spirits, and despite the graffiti found throughout the woods, it remains virtually untouched. When vandals hit it, they are isolated instances and the spray-painted writing and paintball hits look more like the work of one or two people.

It is not the most organized or fashionable place. In many ways it looks like a broken down campsite. People find it a calming place, however, a small part of the forest to reflect on spiritual ideas instead of demons and cults. The reservation touches people more profoundly, whether it gives them time to reflect on the calmness of the scene or their own relationship to religion.

There is an odd dichotomy existing on the hundreds of acres set aside for the Wampanoag. On a map, its boundaries are clearly defined by paved and unpaved roads and natural features, but the soul of the place extends beyond, pushing out whatever might be negative. For all of that peace, there is something still unsettling about its place within the forest, like a diamond in the mud or a tree root cracking through the sidewalk. Amongst the beauty of nature and gentle sounds of birds and crickets, the buildings of the reservation are a stark reminder of the uneasy relationship between the town and the Wampanoag.

For the Native Americans who use it, the reservation is much like the summer home Freetown was before the arrival of the British. No one lives there, but rather they travel, sometimes through several states, to attend meetings and religious gatherings. There is no full time staff for the buildings, and there is no authority given to the rangers to protect it.

The buildings therefore are broken down, victims of harsh winters and pounding rains. The damage is not so much from human hands as the forces of nature, hitting the wood over and over again, trying to break the spirit that offers so many people enlightenment. The visitor's center is boarded up, welcoming no one and looking more like the abandon shack of a woodsman. Most of the structures are leftover camps from the CCC, including the main structure used for many of the gatherings they host. It looks like a covered bridge and is filled with old appliances and covered piles of damaged brick and wood. The beams look sturdy, but there is a lived-in feel to them, a moisture coming off them that causes people going through to start scratching. The cracked, concrete floor has grass growing through it in spots, like the forest trying to reclaim what belongs to it.

This is one area where people have seen what they believe is the replay of a ceremony that took place years before they arrived at the forest.

"I stepped back to another time," says Gabe when asked about the ceremony. "They didn't belong here. I don't think they minded us being there, if they knew we were there at all, but they weren't of the twenty-first century."

Gabe and his wife were driving along the edge of the woods, trying to figure out where one of the entrances was, in the summer of 2000, when they noticed the sign marking the Reservation. They drove to the visitor's center and parked the car. Immediately, they knew something was odd.

"We heard the drums as we got out of the car. It was weird. We didn't hear anything, even when our windows were down, but as soon as we got out, the drums started. My wife had been studying Native American traditions and religion, so she wanted to see if there was a powwow going on."

The stage where drums were heard and unexplained smoke appeared.

They followed the sound to the meeting place, noticing the drums getting louder as they approached. Gabe describes the day as slightly overcast, but with no rain expected, yet despite summer temperatures everywhere else, they both began to feel cool, like they had hit a wall of wind.

"They got louder. The drummers were getting faster and there was the sound shoes make when they kick up sand on cement, but there was no one there. We turned the corner, but there wasn't a soul in the place."

The phantom drums continued, and Ilene noticed something odd in the corner. "Right in the corner, there were five columns of smoke. They looked like dark rain clouds, but the height of a person. They weren't moving or anything. They were just there."

Gabe was scared and wanted to run, but Ilene grabbed his hand and slowly escorted him back to the car.

"To her, there was something spiritual. I was scared as hell, but she thought we had disturbed a meeting of sacred energy and she wanted to be respectful. She felt honored to see it, but I wanted nothing to do with it."

While Ilene felt enlightened by what she had witnessed, Gabe was not so soothed. Until that moment, he had not believed in ghosts, and to him, the five spirits in the corner had not been positive. He felt they were separate from the drummers, drawn to them for some reason and observing them. He also felt they were watching him and his wife as they came into view.

There are several reports throughout the forest of a known haunting or a report of monsters accompanied by a dark human-like figure. Popular media has named them shadow people, but their existence is almost always tied to other supernatural occurrences. In most cases, these shadow people are described as being male and having less form than the ghosts seen around them. Many believe these dark men to be a form of demon or negative, nonhuman spirit that finds other paranormal spots and feeds off the energy they produce or attract. The more negative spirit they are feeding off of, the darker and more solid the figure. They have been seen more in recent years, begging the question; are people noticing more or does their appearance mark something else?

Gabe might have been frightened by what he saw at the stage, but others have walked the area and felt a very positive feeling come over them.

It is easy to assume the change is from a sense of tranquility there, but it is something much different.

Tim felt the woods actually spoke to him. He had been having a bad week when he walked through the forest in the fall of 2004. He had been disciplined at work for a dumb mistake he had made and his girlfriend asking him to move out, he'd connected the two somehow—even going so far as to think there was a curse on him. As his bank account went down and his prospects slowly faded, he needed air to sort out his thoughts and escape the world. Living in Fall River, he had spent time in the forest and had gone with his friends to the reservation. When he was younger, they would try to sneak in and watch ceremonies and had once gone there at night with flashlights and a book of Native American legends. They had all left, and they had never seen anything before, but Tim remembered the place as being very quiet.

That was just what he needed, and as he rode his bike out to the spot, thinking about the mistake he had made at work.

"It wasn't like me at all. It was stupid, but my mind was on anything but work. I remember I was rolling around in my head whether I even wanted to stay at my job. Just after the center, there is a circle of rocks. It looks like a big figure eight with stones all around it. I was sitting on the ground, not noticing the flies eating me alive, just thinking."

Tim, who describes himself as a very non-spiritual person, remembers looking at his watch and noting it was three-thirty, almost time to go home. He closed his eyes, but could still hear the birds nearby and feel the wind blowing against his face. At no time, he claims did he fall asleep and he was not praying or looking for guidance.

"I heard this voice. It was a deep male voice and he was speaking in a foreign language. The only thing I can relate it to is when they have Indians speaking in movies."

His feet began to tingle and he felt a hand on his shoulder. Although he did not understand the words, he felt them. "I had never felt that before. I can't understand it, but my life became clear right in that moment. I can't remember what I understood even, but I was jarred to do something different."

The whole experience took only a minute or two, but when Tim finally opened his eyes, it was after five o'clock and the sun had almost set. He went in the next day and gave his notice, even though he had no job lined up and no money to afford a new apartment. Over the next few months, the tumblers began to fall for him. He moved in with a friend, got a better paying job, and eventually found a woman he proposed to in the spring of 2006. He credits his time at the reservation for the turnaround, and while he cannot explain anything that happened that afternoon, he knows something beyond himself intervened and showed him a different path.

The Wampanoags now using the forest find it a deeply spiritual location. The site is used for business, but it is also a place where they can come together as a community and share a piece of themselves. Unlike other sacred grounds, there is both a secular and a holy purpose for the setting. Even those people who are not from this area or who do not share ancestors with the Native Americans from Freetown feel the power. Perhaps some of this is left behind after the ceremonies are finished. There may be energy left by those who pray there. Many of the religious ceremonies call upon the leaders who have died to communicate with them and offer them guidance. There may be a direct line open now and a non-Wampanoag in need can find his way there as well.

Alice feels she is connected to that line, too, but her experience, while positive, left her wanting less proof of life after death. The stories of the potential of the reservation made it an ideal location for a Wiccan prayer service she was planning. She is a solitary practitioner, gaining most of her knowledge from books and websites, but to her, the religion was more about listening to nature than actually tapping into forces she could manipulate.

Gathering some branches nearby, she built a small alter and began whispering short prayers she had written. They spoke mostly of opening herself up and experiencing the power around her, and as she continued under her breath she got the feeling she was being watched. Instead of a general sense, she felt the eyes on one side of her and then on the other. She was growing more scared and decided to leave, but before she did she had to bless and reopen her circle and disassemble her alter, all of which felt like it was taking hours.

She had just finished when she saw the figure of a young boy walking in the field about thirty feet in front of her, hands held out, skipping over the grass. Alice says the boy looked to be about fourteen, and had short hair. He was wearing brown pants, which she says looked like dirty khakis, and no shirt, but what she really noticed was the green light all around him. He was solid, but there was something about him that did not belong in this world.

As he walked, the grass did not move and there was no sound at all. He looked at her, smiled, and turned away. As he walked away, he slowly faded until there was nothing left of him.

Looking back on the experience now, Alice feels moved by what she saw that day. She had left the forest at almost a run, leaving several books and material she had brought behind, but now wishes she had tried to talk to him or had followed him into the field.

There are many things at the reservation not fully understood by those who do not use it. A large circular structure made of logs and dried-out branches appears to be used as a gathering place. There are homemade benches and wood stumps set out around it and flashes of light and quick movements out of the corner of the observer's eyes have been seen there. There are several stone structures, not more than rocks piles together, but there is no logic to their placement near the main buildings. One of the oddest sites at the reservation is the small pile of branches placed on the paths leading from the main reservation out to the woods. Measuring no more than a foot in width, they are made out of intertwined braches tied together to form a square or arranged like Lincoln Logs. They may be used to light fires, but again, they are not part of the main ceremonial area and are placed in random spots.

Not all encounters are profound or even understood. Two different people have experienced a man they describe as looking like a Native

American but who wears jeans and a black t-shirt. Both were looking around the visitor's area when he appeared and asked if he could help them. When they asked when the center would be open, he shrugged and asked if they had seen the fireplace in the woods. They followed his hand to where he was pointing, but when they looked back, he had disappeared.

The fireplace itself is an unusual thing to see in the middle of the woods. Originally used in the CCC days, it looks as out of place now as a burnt-out car. Made of stone and cement, it is covered with vegetation, another example of the forest reclaiming itself. There have been several reports of

smoke coming from the stack when no fire was lit and of observers seeing wood burning inside that mysteriously disappeared when they approached.

Not all of the ghosts at the Reservation are human. Perhaps as a part of Wampanoag spirituality, there have been numerous reports of phantom animals seen in and around several of the spaces near the main area. Seeing animals in the State Forest is not unusual. There are many species of animals not yet classified, and places within the Bridgewater Triangle have a history of unexplained beasts. But the encounters people describe defy even the usual supernatural explanations. They instead paint a picture of a lost moment trapped.

The visitor's center

"I've hunted before," says Adam, a frequent hiker on the trails within the Freetown Forest. "I know what it looks like when an animal gets hit. This deer was not supposed to be there and it died right in front of me." The problem with Adam's story is that the animal could not be found after it was hit and there was no one alive in the woods with him.

One winter morning in late February of 2002, he was walking through the woods near the reservation taking pictures. He was stunned to see a deer cross twenty feet in front of him. The animal did not react to him, but instead, stopped and began picking at the snow. Adam noticed the deer was almost translucent, like a picture being projected against the trees. The animal also had an orange glow around it and made no sound as it went through the snow.

"I wish I had had a gun with me. I sometimes spend three days trying to find a deer like this." Instead Adam grabbed his camera and focused, but as he prepared to shoot, the animal disappeared. "I didn't even think to take the picture. I mean, I don't believe in ghosts, so why would I take a picture of something that's not there."

Adam decided to leave, packing up his camera and lighting a cigarette. As he turned, he saw the animal come out of the woods from the same location and move the exact same way, leaning down to poke at the snow. It was as if he were seeing a replay of the entire experience. If the whole scene was confusing, what happened next left Adam wondering if the animals he had hunted and killed so freely had a soul.

"Something hit it. I saw it jerk like it had been shot, try to run away and then fall. Then it disappeared again." When Adam walked to the spot, he noticed no tracks, blood, or evidence any animal had even been there. By the reaction of the animal, whatever hit it came from his general direction, but he heard no gunshot and saw no arrow hit the deer.

"I think it was my fault. That animal was killed a long time ago, and for some reason it's trapped there. It took me, a hunter, to see it die again."

While it was not a positive experience, it forced Adam to reevaluat his stance on hunting. While he still believes hunters have the right to kill deer, he no longer tracks them himself.

There is another aspect to the energy of the reservation. While so many places in the forest, especially ones easily accessible, have been the sight of crimes, there have been few (if any) reports of that kind of activity from the reservation. There have been only a few reports of dumping there as well. It is as if the criminals stay away or are not attracted to it. It could be the locale is protected by something other than state and federal law.

CHAPTER 5

THE MAN IN THE ROAD

There have been many reports of zombies walking the paths in the forest, and Pukwudgies and Native American ghosts have been seen on the paths and unpaved roads, but there is another roadside haunting which rears its head when sitting down to talk about the supernatural in the State Forest. It is hard to say whether they are true hauntings or just stories built up by the imagination. In the paranormal world, there are

One of the many roads within the forest where people have seen a mysterious man in the road.

things that remain unexplained and unable to be proven, but when they stray from the road a bit and mirror established urban legends, it might be safer to classify them as more fable than fact.

In 1996, two men were driving down Slab Bridge Road along the border of the forest when they saw a male figure in the middle of the road. They hit their brakes, but not before driving over the man. They heard and saw no impact, but stopped the car without pulling to the side of the road. When they got out to investigate the scene, they found no body or blood and decided it was their imagination. They returned to the car, but as they approached, the front headlights turned on, blinked twice, and then shut off. The car was not running at the time, and the keys were in the driver's jacket pocket.

The two men were unable to give a description of the person they believed they hit other than to say it was a tall man, at least six feet, with short hair and dark shirt on.

Another driver claims she saw a man in the road on Bell Rock Road between two cemeteries. It was daylight and she was listening to her favorite talk radio show. She admits to not paying attention to the road in front of her until she saw a man with short hair and a brown shirt in front of her car. He was holding his hands up as if bracing for an impact. She drove through him, feeling a cold chill, and then stopped, almost driving her car off the road. When she turned, there was no man and no evidence the entire thing had happened.

Similar incidents have been reported by other people on different roads inside the forest. Bell Rock Road has the most incidents by far, with sighting on both sides of the town line. In their reports, the man walks into the street before getting hit, although a few have him already standing in the middle of the road. All report running through him and finding nothing when they get out of their cars. It is almost impossible to disappear from sight quickly enough to go undetected, so the man is said to vanish when hit.

There are possible explanations to the stories. People have suffered violent assaults on the roads in the area. Bodies have been dumped, and other attacks have been recorded that might account for a ghost sighting. People believe there are still bodies authorities have yet to find, and these bodies might be found close to the roads. Soldiers from King Phillip's War might remain on the land they gave their lives for, although there is no real evidence of any battles taking place in the forest. Also, the reports never mention the man as wearing old-fashioned clothes. There are several cemeteries along Bell Rock Road, and these might account for anything unexplained.

Of course, they might not be traditional ghosts at all. With so much tragedy in the area, there might be energy left behind. Rather than conscience spirits, they might be psychic recordings playing themselves over and over again. This would make sense given the sheer number of people who took their final drive along these paths.

Sometimes the simplest explanation is the best. There is a long history of these kinds of hauntings, and the majority are more urban legend than paranormal experiences. One of the most well researched tales, and the one that comes up the most as the center of a haunted location, is the ghostly hitchhiker. Every town has their own haunted hitchhiker legend, from the famous Resurrection Mary in Chicago to the Redheaded Hitchhiker of Route 44 in nearby Rehoboth. In that Massachusetts town, the ghost has become such a strong legend, it seems the local sports team would do well to change its name. People are tired of being asked about him, but the reports still come in today, many of which include first-hand stories.

The Man in the Road in Freetown might owe something to these stories. The reports are rarely first hand and are swapped on message boards and e-mails as something that happened to someone the person knows. They almost never happen during the day, and research reveals there is something very powerful about the suggestive nature of driving along a dark and lonely road at night. There are also certain words repeated in the retelling of the story indicating a higher script the person is reading from. The man always has short hair and cannot be described in detail. The man is never seen once the car is stopped and is never seen by people using off-road vehicles or motorcycles, two very popular modes of transportation through the forest.

They almost always use the term impact and skid when talking about the incident. These simple consistencies may reinforce the idea of it being the same ghost, but when compared to other stories told nationally, there are too many details exactly the same.

Former Freetown detective Alan Alves is now a specialist in hypnotics and might offer some clue as to the why behind the strongest haunted urban legend. He describes the conflict between the waking brain and our imaginative brain.

When driving long periods, especially when the mind tends to wander, the imagination part of our brain takes over and guides us. This is how we arrive at our destination and cannot remember how we got there. During this influence, stored ideas hidden within that part of our imagination come out. We are more inclined to see the images we fear and the ghosts of our subconscious. One of the most powerful of these is the image of the roadside man.

For now the Man in the Road will be placed on the far side of local legend, but he remains with one foot planted firmly on the fence of fact.

CHAPTER 6

THE MAD TRUCKER OF COPICUT ROAD

People in the roads are not the only things haunting the dirt and paved streets near the forest. According to the website *New England Legends,* a popular ghost story among the locals of Freetown involves a phantom car. Known as the "Mad Trucker of Copicut Road," the man is said to drive a pickup and flash his lights while blaring his horn at you. The ghost is visibly upset and angry you are there. After trying to run you off the road, he disappears.

This legend is very similar to others in surrounding town. Usually, the man is the killer of a young child in the area and seen in the location of the accident that took the juvenile's life. The Mad Trucker is missing these elements but retains many other aspects. There have been several people who have witnessed this ghost, but none are willing to talk about it on the record for fear of being ridiculed or because they do not want to relive it. They are shaken by what has happened.

CHAPTER 7

THE GHOST OF PROFILE ROCK

Some places are home to solitary ghosts, lone figures trapped in time who appear dark against the landscape, telling everyone they do not belong. They are not the scary monsters out of nightmares, but tragic figures, often replaying the moment of their deaths and inspiring empathy instead of fear. They are unexplained, but more than that, they are physical moments of history, reminding us what once was and forcing us to remember a past we try to put behind us.

The Freetown State Forest is bursting at the seams with violent places. There are monsters in this section and bodies found in that, but one lo cation keeps the spirit of a noble diplomat turned

Courtesy of Jeff Belanger, ghostvillage.com

warrior. Philip, the last leader of the Wampanoags before the dismantling of his nation, once stood high on the rocks there, watching his land slowly slip away. He now returns, unable to let go and still hoping he can somehow keep his people together.

The most recognizable feature within the forest, and perhaps the most noticeable natural landmark in Massachusetts, might be the rock formation on Old Joshua's Mountain. Named after the first permanent settler in the area, Joshua Tisdale, it is the state's own Old Man in the Mountain. Most people in the area know it by its more descriptive name, Profile Rock, and the people who visit there know the man immortalized in the stone attracts spirits the way he once drew in his people.

Although formed by natural means, people have felt for centuries the perfect profile on Joshua's Mountain is that of Massasoit, Wampanoag sachem during the early days of English settlement and father to Alexander and Philip. The fifty-foot-high rock is surrounded by woods on all sides, with paths cut out mostly by foot traffic. The entrance off Slab Bridge Road is accessible to the public, and the park rangers identify it as one of the most popular spots in the area. The rock is not physically within the woods, but the property is now considered part of the State Forest.

Once inside the park, visitors notice the profile as they turn up the rock trail, set off on both sides by medium sized, irregular stones. Bikes and motorcycles often stop off to view the mountain, and from that distance, the face still appears noble, solid, and strong and still watching over the forest.

Despite attempts to keep it clean and restore its beauty, it is still a meeting place for the youth of the town, a place to get drunk and let loose, and the many niches constituting the sides of the mountain make it more attractive to people doing no good. Unlike the Assonet Ledge, a good pair of shoes will allow you to climb from the bottom up to the head of Massasoit, and people have been known to climb halfway up to break off pieces.

History does not tell when Massasoit became connected to Profile Rock, but it is known that the mountain was considered sacred long before the chief came into power. For generations preceding his birth, the Wampanoag met there to discuss tribal issues and to protect themselves against their enemies. It was a vital part of their culture, easily accessible and high enough to see much of the surrounding land. It provided an excellent defense, but there was a positive energy they felt and were attracted to.

Looking back, Massasoit might have felt like a savior to many within his tribe. He kept the people together in the face of disease, tribal warfare, and the English settlers. It is understandable they would associate the stone with him, but it was this recognition that may have trapped his son, Philip, to remain at Profile Rock. After the death of his father, Philip was forced to deal with intensifying problems with the English, other tribes, and his own people. He often came to the mountain to seek guidance. During the war it is said he went to the rock to mediate and meet with his war general, Anawan. No doubt he felt some connection to the place many claimed looked like his father, but he may have also used it to remind the people of his bloodline.

A mysterious prayer or poem written near the base of Profile Rock. *Courtesy of Justin MyCofsky.*

Massasoit had formed a tentative alliance with the English of Plymouth Colony, brokering the peace for decades before his death. He was known as a wise man and a resource, even in the next life, for policy and strategy and would have made a good counselor, even in death. This might account for the reports today of a man sitting in a praying position on the rock. Perhaps the intensity of Philip's prayers there imprinted themselves and we see the fallen sachem replaying his futile attempt to save his people from massacre.

Patrick knew of Profile Rock from an early age. Aside from seeing it on the patches of the police in town, his father would bring him to the mountain when he went to paint landscapes of it. His father would sit for hours, trying to capture the perfect emotion of the place, and Patrick would play with the rocks and try to climb the trees.

"My father was not an artist. He had taken some classes before, but he was a cook. Not at all what you would think of as a painter, but he loved that place." Patrick says his father would talk about being drawn in by the stone, but he could never communicate why. "He felt something there. He painted other things, but he always went back to Profile Rock. I don't think he ever got it right. He didn't know what he felt, he just felt it."

It meant nothing to Patrick to climb the face of the stone. He had done it for as long as he could remember. In late 2001, the climb felt different.

"I think it was the first time I knew what my father felt. All those times with him, I'd always used the place as a playground. That day though, I think I felt what he was trying to say with those paintings."

As he made it way up the rock, carefully placing each foot as he went, he felt the air change around him. It became very warm, almost humid, and he found it hard to breath. He looked up to see someone looking down at him. He said the man had dark skin and no hair. The man extended his arm as if to help Patrick up, but when Patrick looked down to make sure his feet were secure, the man vanished.

"I don't know what I saw, but the whole thing seemed wrong. Well, not wrong as much as out of place. I never felt threatened, but I knew I had seen a ghost."

Rich saw Philip one afternoon while walking his dog back in 1987. He lived nearby and would take Jingle across the street and into the woods. He approached the rock, all the time looking at the profile. A figure slowly appeared, faint at first and then becoming solid. The man was sitting on the top and stood, extending his hands and then bringing them back to his chest. He sat back down and slowly faded away.

"Jingle saw him, too. He can't tell his story, but I know he saw something. He's always moving his head side to side and pulling me forward. I saw that Indian and he [the dog] stopped and just stared at the guy."

Most of the sightings follow the same pattern, and the experience leaves the observer with a profound sense of sadness. They never feel threatened, but they feel they have somehow touched Philip's grief.

It is said Philip spent the night before his death at Profile Rock, maybe even knowing his fate. After early successes in hit and run battles, the Wampanoag were feeling the momentum of the war shift. Philip must have seen this himself, and it is almost certain he knew he would not live much longer if the English continued to win the war. If it was not the next day, eventually he would fall, and the realization of this might have been enough mark the rock with his anxiety.

The story of the hauntings may be the story of two soldiers and their final meeting with each other. It is also said he had a meeting with Anawan right before this, and it might be this meeting connecting the two allies over the centuries.

After Philip's death, Anawan was left to continue fighting, and shortly after he saw no other solution than surrender. He officially submitted to Captain Benjamin Church in Rehoboth, Massachusetts, and was taken prisoner by the English. Although he and his troops were promised amnesty, Anawan was executed upon his arrival in Plymouth. It was the final betrayal in a war that prided itself on backstabbing and atrocities.

The area of Rehoboth where he surrendered became known as Anawan Rock, and has a rich history of folklore and hauntings attached to it. According to Charles Turek Robinson, author of *The New England Ghost Files,* the site has been the subject of rumors almost since Anawan's death. Some residents report seeing lights at night in the swamps near the rock. Chanting and voices have been heard, the most disturbing of which seemed to be saying, "Stand and fight," in an Algonquin language. A fire was also seen burning on the rock and then mysteriously disappearing.

After the publication of the book in 1994, people began traveling to Anawan Rock to see the ghosts for themselves. Local teens often hung around as well, getting drunk and hiding in trees, waiting for the curious to come and then giving them the scare of their lives. Some have come forward with more evidence of activity, but it becomes difficult to sift through the stories once a site is known and well traveled to. Often the lore built up around a spot affects the people looking for ghosts. They see lights because they have been told they should. Pictures get overanalyzed, and any speck of dust becomes the ancient warrior.

There have been other reports from Anawan Rock which seem genuine and truthful. They mostly involve lights and fires, although a few have heard the chanting and drums Robinson describes. One of the more odd reports involves a teenager who hid himself in the woods to scare people on Halloween back in 1998. While waiting for people to show up, he and his friends were driven out of the woods by a large, red ball of light, about the size and shape of a man, which produced an intense heat. Many of the same kinds of reports come from Profile Rock. It does seem the two souls are connected, looking at each other from two battlefields of the war, perhaps trying to warn the other of his fate.

While the anxiety, betrayal, and death both suffered is more than enough to explain any ghost at their rocks, there might be another reason their spirits cannot find rest. It may be this connection that explains the curse which continues to plague both towns.

In another book, *True New England Mysteries, Ghosts, Crimes and Oddities*, Charles Robinson tells the tale of the Wampanoag wampum belt. The belt, a collection of woven beads telling the history of the people, disappeared after the war. The belt stands as the only true history of the Wampanoag, untouched by the Bible or Puritan influence, and its vanishing is symbolic of the Native American of old in New England. Robinson tells how the belt was passed to Anawan and then taken into custody when he was arrested. It fell into the hands of Governor Winslow from Plymouth who sent it back to England as proof of his victory over the Native Americans and his power in the New World. The king never received the prize.

Attempts have been made to trace the history of the belt after its departure from Rehoboth, but none have succeeded. Robinson puts forth several theories to the fate of the artifact, but none have ever been verified and the belt remains missing, destroyed or forgotten in some depository. The history of the Wampanoag remains lost with it.

It has been said Philip may have relinquished the belt to Anawan during one of his meetings at Profile Rock, causing the loss of the history of a people he had sworn to protect. This grief might also force him to perch on his father's head, leaning towards Rehoboth, waiting for the return of the relic. Some have even said the curse of Bristol County might have been sparked by the removal of the Wampanoag wampum belt, and its return is the only thing that will bring peace to the spirits. It seems unlikely the belt will ever be returned, so the secrets held by the ghosts in the forest, and at Profile Rock, will remain hidden.

And Philip will also continue to appear at Profile Rock.

CHAPTER 8

THE DIGHTON ROCK MYSTERY

Not all of the mysteries of the forest involve ghost and monsters. Some are as natural as the rocks themselves. Perhaps the most notorious boulder in Massachusetts makes its new home just over the border from Freetown. Its past is not just written in stone, but in an unknown language that has intrigued and baffled scientists for decades. It remains a tourist attraction for the curious and the ambitious, but those who travel there never find the answers they are looking for. It is a landmark claimed by different cultures, all of whom have something essential to read from its surface, but true ownership may never be fully claimed. It is the link to someone's past, but discovering whose time line it connects has so far been impossible. It might be a key to understanding the curse existing in Freetown, but the rock is not talking to anyone.

Dighton Rock makes it home in Berkeley, Massachusetts, but is under the watchful eye of the same people who maintain the forest. The small building housing the massive stone is an extension of the forest, although no formal link to the two exists. The forty-ton formation of mica and feldspar made its way to the mouth of the Taunton River over ten thousand years ago and landed in Bristol County upside down. The first official sketch of its surface was made by Dr. John Danforth around 1680, only a few years after King Philip's War. He only examined half of the stone, but his discovery raised questions. Several years later it was written about as one of the marvels of Massachusetts by Cotton Mather in his book, *Curiosa*.

The people who discovered Dighton Rock were not consumed by its physical features but by the ten by four foot west-facing surface. The stone contains markings that have been the source of tension and mystery since the days of its first discovery. It is said to be the oldest inscribed rock in Massachusetts, maybe even in the country, and it points to an earlier settlement in the area. Columbus did not come to Bristol County, but someone before him might have left their mark on the small towns there.

The markings on the stone are a collection of pictures, letters and symbols that paint a mixed picture of who might have been the first to carve it. Over the years many cultures have looked into it, all of whom find meaning in their language among the etchings. It has been attributed to the English, the Vikings, the Italians, and the Native Americans. Danforth was partial to the Native American theory when he first found it. To him, it showed a great battle between the Wampanoags and some travelers who had made their way down the Taunton River. This theory is dismissed today. Not only did he see only part of the drawings, but it is known the Native Americans did not use formal numbers or letters, both of which are clear on the surface.

The predominate theory about the writing on Dighton Rock is that it is of Portuguese origin. Although this may seem convenient in a community with a high concentration of Portuguese immigrants, there is evidence to support their claim. At least one of the numbers on the rock appears to be the date 1511 in a unique Portuguese font. Other markings seem to be the national symbols of Portugal and a symbol which resembles the Portuguese Cross of the Order of Christ.

Perhaps the most convincing evidence is the name of Miguel Corte-Real on the stone. He was a Portuguese explorer from the sixteenth century who sailed for the New World but never returned. He had traveled to the Americas searching for his missed brother and was never heard from again. Might Corte-Real have followed rumors of his brother's whereabouts or gotten blown off course and traveled up the river, eventually finding his way to Dighton and Berkeley? It would seem unlikely he would get lost or travel that far inland without a reason. Not only was he an experienced captain, but his family had been part of the exploration since the early days of his countries efforts. Why than would he go up the river?

The Portuguese theory has gained more strength in recent years, although there is no record of what might have happened to Corte-Real and his ship. The theory of his trip was embraced by people in the region, but also by Portugal itself, especially Corte-Real's hometown of Lisbon, who want nothing more than to lift him up to hero status.

The story of Dighton Rock picks up in the twentieth century. After discovering the possible link to Portuguese culture in 1918, the push began to preserve the rock and protect it from the world it had fought against for so long. In 1954, the land around the rock was purchased by a group of people from New York to preserve the stone in honor of its Portuguese lineage. This became the foundation of the current park where

Dighton Rock is kept. The rock was removed from the water and given a place of honor, in a way, on land for all to see. Unfortunately, it was protected by a small fence and not well supervised or properly protected. In 1973, the rock was moved again, this time indoors to a new protected building. It had found its final resting place after ten thousand years of rolling and lifting. In 1974, the Massachusetts Legislature, under Chapter 501, House Bill number 5475, created the Dighton Rock Museum to not only protect and honor the stone, but also to give the people the full story, with all theories, and allow them to decide.

Today, the museum is open to the public in the summer and houses several other artifacts from the explorers of the time. It stands as a testament of the dedication of Portuguese immigrants and a symbol of commitment to the past.

There are a few reports of paranormal activity at the rock, and there are no real credible ones worth reporting. The one legend attached to the area is of a mysterious man who is sometimes seen walking around the outside by people trying to get into the building at night. He is seen as only a thick shadow and runs away when called to. This story, however, was posted on a local message board with no first hand reports and no follow up stories attached to it.

Dighton Rock does have its place in the supernatural story of the Freetown State Park. It offers another path to walk down when looking at the mysterious history of the area. While Miguel Corte-Real, or someone from his ship, is widely accepted as the etcher of the stone, it still is not confirmed or fully understood. The mystery of why he was on the Taunton River has yet to be explained. Perhaps he was drawn in by the same forces manifesting themselves in other ways in the Bridgewater Triangle and Freetown. Perhaps there is another answer to the Dighton Rock question, and that answer might be the key to understanding what is happening in the cursed county. Whether it is buried under the ice, exposed to the river and elements, or housed inside a museum, Dighton Rock still keeps some of its history to itself.

CHAPTER 9

LIGHTS FROM THE LEDGE

Courtesy of Jeff Belanger, ghostvillage.com

Mitchell had just come off a shift at a local retail store where he worked to make a little spending cash for college. Like most of his friends that summer, he worked during the day and hung out at night, and with little to do in town, he went to the Ledge in the forest to see who was there. Several people he knew were already sitting high on the rock, drinking and playing music on their portable radio. He had a few beers, flirted a little, and laughed about some stupid customers who had come in during the day. He was far from drunk when he got up and walked over the edge of the cliff.

"I can remember laughing and having fun. We were all just sitting there. Some people drinking, some smoking a little, but no one was angry or getting in anyone's face. I had done it a hundred times. A thousand." Mitchell remembers starting to feel depressed and overwhelmed by a feeling of loneliness. As he got closer to the edge he started to sense the others were laughing at him.

"I felt like I should jump. The world was against me and nothing was going right. I mean, it wasn't true. I'm generally a happy guy, but the thoughts made complete sense. I wanted to kill myself. Two minutes earlier I was laughing. Now I wanted to jump. It didn't make any sense, but it was real."

A friend called out and he snapped out of his trance. He walked back to the group, told a few more jokes and then walked back to his car still trying to figure out where the thoughts of suicide had come from. "I don't know what would have happened if I had done that. It wasn't me. I've never been back there since."

Mitchell's experience is not uncommon in the area of the forest known as the Ledge. For generations, it has been a place to hang out, whether it is late at night and you have a few beers around or it is daytime and you have a fishing pole and some new lures. It is one of the most naturally beautiful sections of the forest, but it is also the most haunted. An echo remains there from tragedies from another time, a grief trapped in the stone and water waiting for a player to reenact an event so emotional its energy cannot be freed. The Ledge is haunted, and with each new victim the legend surrounding it grows.

The Ledge, officially known as the Assonet Ledge, has been a favorite spot for people in the forest for years. Formed millions of years ago, it was hallowed out by constant digging during its years as a quarry. The once almost level stone now drops off into a deep pool of water below. Found in the southeastern section of the forest, not far from the Fall River line, it can be a peaceful spot favored for its fishing and view of the forest. There are two roads leading to it that circle at the top and meet at the bottom, Upper Ledge Road and Ledge Road. Neither is fully paved and they are often washed out, creating large ravines that make traveling with a car difficult. Someone standing on the top looking down can see anyone who might be coming, making it a favorite spot for the youth in town who are trying to find trouble.

The stone is made from rock known as arkoses granite, which contains feldspar and hornblende. This makes the stone very dense, heavy, and hard to work with. Nevertheless, large stones were removed by the Fall River Granite Company and used to make buildings all over southern New England. The cliff overlooking the quarry is between fifty and sixty feet tall with jagged rock formations leading to the water. The distance to the bottom of the pond has never been measured, but it is estimated to be about seventy feet deep. The water is so cold professional divers asked to look for evidence during a criminal investigation refused to go back in after spending time close to the bottom.

Although the site is well known, at night the sanctuary is far away from the eyes of the normal people who visit the forest. Gone are the families looking for a day out and the motorcycles cutting through the peace of the trees. When the partiers are away and there is a moment of silence, the Ledge might as well be another part of the word in a different time. That might have been the appeal in the early days of the Wampanoag.

Courtesy of Jeff Belanger, ghostvillage.com

Someone at the rock is rarely alone though. Teenagers use the spot for parties. Most claim there is nothing to do but hang out and get drunk, and like many youth, they find a common area to do it. Jumping off is far from a suicide wish. The water might be cold, but it offers a cushion to anyone with enough sense to leap from the right portion of the cliff. Going over from the top is dangerous, but climbing down to the second level, a trick in and of itself, makes the feat doable, especially with a few in you and your friends egging you on. Most do it at night, and several have claimed to have done it many times.

Jumping is not the only thing going on up at the top of the Ledge. The stone is completely covered with graffiti, most along the lines of "Jack loves Jill" and bands people listen to. Over the years the writing has changed. Whether only curious youth or actual practitioners, the stone has been a canvas for Satanic and occult markings. People have sensed the power of the stones and conducted rituals there, often resulting in burn marks in the crevices of the rock. Most feel it is just kids fooling around, but there are other signs something more involved might be happening there. Cult authorities have analyzed the writing and found hidden codes, directions to other areas in the forest and messages to other groups.

According to Steven Bates, the head of the ranger department for Freetown, the graffiti is a nuisance, but harmless. In his years there, he has seen it come and go, and his office has made a special effort to clean the place up. Recently, they brought in special environmentally safe blasting equipment and washed the writing away. He admits his efforts seem useless at times. "It's like we just cleaned the slate so they could graffiti it."

He believes there is no more occult marking there, but a closer look at the tags show activity has just become more secretive. The path leading to the top of the Ledge has *666* written in fresh blue paint, and the same color used in several other bizarre pictures and messages in the same area, including the word, "Homicide" and "Kill Kill Kill."

"I saw some a few months ago," says Sue, a local teen. She claims her and her friends were planning on going up, but when they arrived at the bottom they saw a fire and several people dressed in what looked like robes. "It's the going joke. If you see them, find another place to party."

A bigger problem for forest authorities is the constant dumping at the Ledge. People have been known to dump cars, bikes and motorcycles, and household appliances off the top or push them out the back of their trucks at the bottom. Although the practice is not as common as it was a few years ago, trash can still be seen bobbing in the water, caught in rocks so only small sections are above the surface. People who visit say the dumping is unfortunate, but they go about their business as if it is not there.

The energy at the Ledge goes deeper than just kids with spray cans and illegal dumping. Death has visited the Ledge, and people who frequent there today can still feel the sorrow of those who were killed or chose suicide among the stone.

The Wampanoags speak of avoiding the area all together. Several have reportedly been killed there over the years, either by falling or by drowning in the water below. The deaths are unexplained and not always attributed to suicide. Something pushed them. One of the explanations might be the demons known as the Pukwudgie. They are said to lure people to the edge and then push them off. Sometimes they use bright balls of light, thought to be the souls of departed tribesman, to get them to walk over themselves.

Some of the Native American deaths occurred at their own hands. To escape capture and torture during the King Philip's War, they jumped from the top rather than surrender. Their war cries are heard by people who visit there, as if in trying to find peace, they only invited an eternity of living their final moment.

In 1997, Darren was fishing with his brother and a good friend of his in the quarry when they saw what they believed were the ghosts of some of these Wampanoags. "We spotted movement on the top right hand side of the Ledge and it seemed there were about six to eight people hiding behind trees and bushes." As the three of them watched, the men disappeared. For the next minute or so, they looked on as the men appeared in random places, making their way to the bottom. Each time they disappeared and reappeared somewhere else, something that defies reason because the cliff drops straight down and someone would have to climb from one foothold to another. "The sun was setting and it was starting to get darker, so we couldn't make out who they were and we couldn't even make out what they were wearing, if they were wearing anything at all." This made Darren and his friend assume they were Native Americas, especially given the short distance between the Ledge and the main area of the reservation.

The three friends were spooked, especially when they could not find the men again, and jumped into their truck. They drove in a circle but were unable to find anyone. What Darren remembers the most about the occurrence was the men seemed to not have faces. They talked about it for a while after and all agreed on what they had seen. It must have been the ghosts of Native Americans from the area.

While Darren and the others swear to what they have seen, it might be a case of an urban legend or expectation tainting their vision. While it is possible some Native Americans might have died in the area, the reports may very well be exaggerated. Until the blasting and hauling began, there was no ledge at the Assonet Ledge. The rock dropped off, but at no where near the height of today. It is possible there could have been an accident or a Pukwudgie attack and someone might have died from the jagged rock, but there is no way they would have drown after jumping into the water from the top. There was no water there.

Other ghosts at the Ledge do not owe their origin to urban legend, but rather have become the subject of myth. The deaths inspiring the ghost are anything but the subject of rumor but have been transformed over time. Several people have killed themselves by tossing their bodies from the rock. As stated before, the Ledge is not a straight drop, but rather the face is uneven with parts sticking out and flat surfaces to land on. Someone wanting to hurt themselves could easily fall off the wrong section and never be heard from again. There have been dozens of fatal jumps reported over the years, although very few can be confirmed. The odd thing about the jumpers is their state of mind. Some came to the forest to die, while others entered of sound mind. An internet chatroom posting from early 2005, claimed to be from the friend of a man who went in with his girlfriend. They enjoyed a picnic during an overcast summer day. He went to relieve himself nearby and as he started back he saw his girlfriend frown, wave, and then jump to her death. She had been smiling only moments before and had no history of depression.

While this story cannot all be verified and may be the anonymous words of someone looking for attention, there have been people who have killed themselves there. In 2004, a man from Fall River with no history of depression jumped and killed himself in front of his friends and girlfriend. All there agreed he had jumped and had not fallen or slipped. Locals, using word of mouth and the internet, have created lore around the deaths, inflating the mystic of the quarry and making it hard to distinguish between urban legend and truth.

One such legend involves a woman who jumped after losing the man she loved. It might sound like typical folklore, but many in Freetown and the surrounding towns believe it. It has all the elements of a good story, which usually makes a tale too good to be true. A woman had planned to meet her lover at the Ledge for a midnight tryst. The two families did not get along, or the man was not liked by her father. They were set to meet at midnight, and when the man did not show up for several hours after that, the woman assumed she had fallen out of favor with her beloved and tossed herself into the water below.

Since the suicide, her ghost has been seen at the Ledge, still waiting in sorrow for the man to show up. A few have claimed to see her reenact her death. From water level, they see her appear at the top and jump, hitting the water and disappearing without causing a splash. Some have jumped into the frigid water to try and save her, but she is never seen again.

Radio talk show host Matt Moniz claims he saw the woman in the early nineties while arriving with some friends late at night. He noticed a woman standing near the edge just out of the woods to his left. Knowing people often came to the spot, he did not think twice. When he looked back at her a second later she was gone. He glimpsed her for only a moment and cannot offer a description except to say she was shadowy and he could tell she was a woman because he noticed she had breasts in profile. Moniz claims there was little light, but the form was definitely a person and he had not been drinking or impaired in any way.

Moniz also claims there is nowhere the woman could have gone. She was at least ten feet from the woods, and an examination of the rock proved she could not have stepped down out of sight without carefully climbing down the stone. When he mentioned what he had seen to his friends, he was surprised by their response. They all knew of the legend and retold her story. Moniz had never heard it himself but claims it was common knowledge among people from Freetown.

The themes of the story are familiar to people who study urban legends and folklore. Two lovers, separated for some reason, agree upon a meeting. One does not show up, almost always because of a misunderstanding, and the other commits suicide. The spirit is cursed to remain on the spot. In the most romantic retellings, the ghost can only be set free by reuniting with the soul of the lost lover. It is worth noting many of these tales involve water, most a bridge or cliff.

The story is an old one, and if it sounds familiar, it is because it has been borrowed and used in stories for centuries. Dracula's wife killed herself by jumping from a window to the water below, upon hearing the false tale of his death, encouraging him to become cursed. Shakespeare has used the theme several times, most notably in the ultimate tale of youthful passion, *Romeo and Juliet*. Modern tales have added the twist of the ghost returning, and it has been recycled enough to become familiar, even to those who might not believe in ghosts. There are no wooden bridges in Vermont that have not been the scene of a lover's suicide.

It would appear the true sightings in Freetown have again encouraged the story to stick to whatever might haunt the Ledge. No suicide of a young woman can be confirmed that might be a good candidate for the specter, but people claim it happened decades ago, so any records one might find would probably not include her reasons.

People who study the paranormal are not entirely discouraged when a haunting they hear of echoes an urban legend. People need to make sense out of their experiences, and one of the most disorienting and intimidating experiences one can have is a paranormal encounter. They cannot put the pieces together, but if they can relate it to a popular story, it makes it easier to digest. Others have experienced the same thing, or there might be an excellent reason for what they have seen. In a small way, the world makes sense again.

There are stories not told about the souls trapped under the water. Some victims might never have shown up in the paper or had a proper burial. Law enforcement believes the water of quarry might hold bodies never found. The temperature of the water and the difficulty in getting to the bottom make it the perfect dump spot for any criminal entering the forest. Anyone weighted down might sink to the bottom and never be found.

Different people have reported seeing lights in the water they associate with the spirits of those trapped below. This too might be explained away. Planes overhead or moonlight catching the minerals in the rock might make the glow people describe, but to those who see it, the lights can not be rationalized and are often accompanied by other paranormal experiences.

Cindy was at the top with several friends one night in 2003. She had been drinking with them when the night started but had stopped a few hours before the occurrence. They were all looking over the edge, daring each other to jump, when she noticed an odd orange light from underneath the water.

"I couldn't tell how big it was because the water was so far away. It just kept getting bigger, like it was coming up from the water. It looked like it was swimming to the top." She says it stopped before it reached the surface and sunk back down, almost as if someone had tried to make it out and had given up. As it faded, she heard a woman scream and a splash, although no one saw any disturbance in the water.

Although she has seen several other unexplained things in the forest, she said she was most moved by the lights. All of them saw the glow, and after the mood changed, Cindy described it as a sudden sadness. They disbanded and all went home.

Tragedy does find its way to the Ledge. During its days as a quarry, there was a blacksmith shop onsite to make the materials needed to blast and process the rock. According to a member of the Freetown Historical Society, the entire quarry shut down after a horrific event. It seems the blacksmiths were working with explosives too close to the dynamite used to break up the stone. It ignited and blew up a section of the shop, killing several men and forcing the company to close production. Although there have been no sightings linked to this occurrence, it further proves the magnetism the location has for bad things and offers another theory on who the balls of light might be.

With so many ghosts making themselves known, and so many different kinds of specters being seen or felt, it begs the question: Who and what are the ghosts at the Ledge?

None of the ghosts sighted at the Ledge interact with the viewer. Some are seen on the top, like the one Matt Moniz saw, and do not notice the people around them. The ones seen jumping do not even cause a splash in the water. The Native Americans seen by Darren looked at them and were making their way down the rock towards them, but it might be more the three men were scared of the unexplained and only felt they were being attacked.

This points towards the most common type of haunting: the psychic recording. This involves the energy of a tragic event, one that would release powerful emotions, becoming trapped in an environment. The right conditions and the event replays itself for modern people to see. Think of a scream being heard at the same time every night in a haunted house. Nothing is seen and nothing else happens, but the screaming continues. Enough of an emotional event or enough energy created, and the imprint might take the form of an actual person, unable to communicate, but acting out the tragedy for eternity.

The science of this type of haunting is only theoretical, but it has everything to do with energy and the principle of all matter changing form instead of being created or destroyed. If energy can be trapped and seen years later, the Ledge would be the ideal situation.

Moniz is firm in what he saw, but he also has a scientific explanation for the activity at the Ledge. He has been a paranormal investigator for more than a decade, but his training is as a scientist. During the day his feet are firmly planted in his day job, and he brings this understanding of the scientific method and the natural order of the world to his investigations. According to him, the combination of quartz, other minerals, and water creates an electromagnetic reaction that releases and attracts energy. It might be this energy that traps spirits in the spot or makes the present paranormal energy intensify for the witness. He also admits it might have an effect on people's physiology, causing slight hallucinations and even the emotional changes connected to the suicides.

The boundaries of the forest might not be enough to contain the power of the Ledge. For years the granite there was quarried and used in buildings throughout the northeast. They were carried out by railcar and the tracks can still be seen on the other side of Route 24. Several of these buildings are haunted in their own right. Some of the stone was used in making the grand mansions in Newport. Although it is unclear which ones received the stone, most have a strong haunted history. Fort Adams, also in Newport, was said to have been built using the same material and has its own ghostly legends drawing people every Halloween. In Massachusetts, one of the most haunted buildings in the state, the Taunton State Hospital, is made from Freetown granite. It would seem any curse on the land follows it when it leaves the forest.

Like many things in Freetown, you can struggle with a question of the chicken or the egg. After you forget the useless question of whose spirits might be at the Ledge, you are still left with the negative energy many feel. People have killed themselves without reason due to the power of the sadness. Is that sadness, that intangible emotion so many have claimed is present, the grief of the past or has it always been there? Has tragedy been draw there, like so many other locations through-out the woods, or did a single event trigger the energy and each addition violent act feeds what is already there? Do the cults who regularly meet there feel something more than we do, or do their actions raise something supernatural at rest?

Regardless of the answers, people continue to visit the Ledge. Some go to fish and swim during the day, while others drink, graffiti, and practice their religion. It is still a place to meet, the same way it was centuries ago. In the same way, it is also the meeting place of every rationalization of the supernatural people come into contact with. Odd geology and chemistry mix with urban legend and rumor, giving bystanders a reason to shake their heads. The legends and stories continue to grow, and visitors have their own stories to tell. Most are not scared by their experiences but in-stead feel a connection to the melancholy cycling through. It would seem the Assonet Ledge, one of the most heartbreaking haunted spots in the for-est, inspires sympathy instead of terror.

CHAPTER 10

ZOMBIES

Zombies are the unexplained among the unexplained. They are more monster than human and more human than ghost, lumbering through the dark parts of cemeteries and the lost places of the world looking for something they will never find. Wandering aimlessly but with odd purpose, they inspire nightmares of lost peace after death, and seeing one can cause the viewer to question their faith in a higher being and contemplate the true meaning of the soul.

In the strictest, accepted sense, a zombie is a living person, but the nature of this beast goes far beyond that simple description. The word zombie comes from the African word zumbi meaning, "departed spirit," and was adopted by Haitian practitioners of Voodoo as they changed continents. Depending on the validity of the witchcraft involved, a zombie was either a person who had been robbed of his soul to act as a slave to the witchdoctor or a person who had been paralyzed using natural anesthetic by the same witchdoctor and buried alive. In the case of the latter, the zombie, who is assumed dead, is brought back by the magician. This suggestion would be as strong as a genuine spell and the effect of the drugs on the subject upon walking would convince the person they were empty, tainted somehow, causing their complete submission.

The legends and media influences surrounding them make identifying a true one nearly impossible. Most reports are of something or some-

The view from the parking lot where a car was attacked by a zombie.

one who acts in an odd way and who fits into the classic movie monster mold. The sighting could be something entirely different, but the observer pulls from their frame of reference and cries zombie. If reports are true, they roam the forest in Freetown, and unlike other supernatural elements in the woods, they have no fear of coming in direct, physical contact with the living.

Of the dozen or so reports of zombies in the forest over the past few years, there are some things that remain constant. The person may be a man or a woman, old or young, wearing clothes from any period, but they all look as if they have just dug themselves out of the ground. They are covered in dirt and often dust rises from their body as they lumber forward. This is the living's first sign something is odd, and is usually enough to make them run as fast as they can to get away. Like in the movies, regardless of the speed of the person trying to escape, the zombie seems to have superior knowledge of the terrain and takes the shortest path to catch up to them again without changing their speed.

Karen and her friend were walking off one of the paths in the forest, looking for unusual birds and taking pictures. Their conversation eventually turned to ghosts. "We had both lived here our whole lives and we knew the reputation of the forest. It was just getting dark and we were scaring each other and challenging each other to stay after the sunset."

As they talked, a man walked out of the woods about fifty yards in front of them just as the path began to curve. "It was already getting dark, and we knew the place wasn't safe for two women, ghosts or no ghosts." She describes the man as being of Latino descent, a little over six feet tall and covered in dirt. He originally walked away from them, but turned after a few steps. Karen noticed his clothes were ripped and looked, "like something from the early 1900s." He was wearing no shoes and made no sound coming out of the woods or on the dirt and twigs as he started towards them.

Both women started to walk back towards the entrance, slow at first, but speeding up as they looked back and saw he was still walking in their direction. "He limped as he walked," Karen says. "The woods are loud at that time of the day. I can't explain it more than that. Everything has a sound, but this man was making no sound." The woman broke into a full sprint, not looking back until they made it back to the car. As they pulled out onto the road, they noticed the same man, now feet from their car, mouth open as he was trying to say something.

"We just drove right by him. There is no way he could have made it back to our car and not have passed us or been seen coming out of the trees somewhere in the parking lot. He was just there."

When they were able to look more closely at him, they both focused on his eyes. "You'd think we wouldn't have looked, but I was drawn to them. They were brown, but had no life in them. They seemed empty, like nothing was going on." Neither women has been back to the forest since, and Karen's friend never talks about what happened. Years after the experience, she still believes the man she saw was not alive.

"Do I have proof? No, just what I felt. I'm interested in ghosts and things, but I don't have an overactive imagination. The thing was dead."

There is plenty to disprove what Karen thought she and her friend saw. Homeless have been known to use the forest in the summer months, and people use the woods as a place to escape for a while or crash in an emergency. Given the crime in the area, someone could have been involved in something illegal, or a camper or hiker could have fallen and was trying to signal for help. For Karen, the only argument she needs for zombies in the trees is her personal experience. Sometimes the gut is a better judge of a situation than the head.

Sheryl has been going to the forest all her life. She and her friends would often take day trips along the trails and broken roads, but her experiences in the forest at night with her friends have stayed with her far longer. She has had many encounters with the unexplained there, but one night in 1985, while driving with her brother and three friends, she ran into a woman she could only describe as a zombie.

A grave dug up and the body removed. A zombie was seen in the woods shortly afterwards, and the grave was then dug up a year later. *Courtesy of Big Operations Productions*

They were parked along the unpaved road miles into the forest. They had done this before, so there was no reason to be afraid. As always, they began joking about some of the things they had seen. Her brother then noticed a woman coming towards them, and while she was not close and was not running, her sudden appearance made them all jump. Sheryl turned on her headlights to get a better look and noticed the woman moved very slowly with no expression on her face.

"The only way to describe her attire is to say that her clothes [looked like they] were buried in dirt for fifty years." Her brother thought the woman looked confused and thought she might be lost. He called to her as she came along side the car.

"Just then she screeched, reached in and grabbed the guy in the back seat by the throat. I hauled butt out of there."

Sheryl was not discouraged or frightened away by the mysterious woman, although she admits of all the things she has seen in the woods, she was most unnerved that night.

Zombies are not unusual in Massachusetts, although most reports seemed to be confused retellings of encounters with something else. In Sheryl's case, what she might have seen was one of the many former mental health patients newly released from a nearby hospital. Around that time, major facilities started to close or reclassify their residents, leading to unhealthy people being let back out into the community. With no means of support and no programs to help after release, hundreds of borderline people found their way to the streets of urban areas and the forests of the more secluded towns.

The task of answering the questions of why and how are even harder than trying to classify a zombie. As a haven for cult activity, there is a chance voodoo practitioners might also be using the forest, and the people seen might have been traditional zombies. Santeria and other forms of voodoo are a religious reality for Cape Verdean, Portuguese, and other immigrant populations that have made the towns in southeastern Massachusetts their home. Investigators have seen evidence of both religions in the forest, as well as items they cannot directly connect, but may represent some offshoot. Bodies are found in the forest, at times in shallow graves, and these deaths might be the result of failed attempts to raise victims. There are also unmarked graves and cemeteries in and near the forest that might account for who these people are.

The other explanation might be in the perception of the witnesses. Most see the zombies at night, and almost all of the reports come from people who frequent the forest and know its reputation. Fear and anxiety might exaggerate the details. They might only be normal people, bloated to the point of myth by scared observers. The mysterious figures in the woods might be odd, but their place in the world of the paranormal remains undefined and unexplained.

CHAPTER 11

THE HAUNTED POLICE STATION

The dark corners of night are prime sources for ghosts to grow. It allows our eyes to see things our minds rationalize in the daytime. If you allow loneliness and a good back story to enter in, the scene is a ghost story waiting to happen. This might be the scenario at the Freetown Police Station, but the people who man the emergency phones during the overnight shift think the fog they see is something more than just a tale spun during the long hours of work. To them it's a coworker.

The police station is a small building on Chase Road, less than a mile from the forest. It's been the site of too many meetings focusing on the dark activity in the forest, but one of its most active cases had nothing to do with a crime. A few years ago, a woman was working the overnight shift manning the radio and emergency lines. Sometime during the night, she died of a heart attack, but because it was a slow night in town, no one noticed she had passed. As the night went on, several officers tried to contact her, but they received no response. Fearing the worst, one officer broke into the station through a window to find her lifeless body.

Since then, several people have complained of an odd fog in the area she died, most often late at night. Looking more like smoke or haze, it stays a moment and then fades away. There is no logical reason for the appearance of the smoke, and it vanishes rather than dissipates. This may be weak grounds to declare it a paranormal event, but those who have witnessed it and retell the story, are people who would have nothing to gain and everything to lose by sharing. They claim it is her spirit, and most find it more intriguing than scary.

Other people report an odd feeling of being watched during that shift. No one during the day has ever seen or felt anything, but that does not take away from the soft voice at least one person claims to have heard at night. The female voice said his name, but he is unsure if it was the woman who had passed, or someone else.

Police in town can confirm the death, but they put little stock in the story of the haunting. Until further information is found, there are only a few eye witness reports to go by as to the nature of the haunting. Whether trapped in the place of her death or returning to her job out of a sense of obligation to the town, she might still be very much still alive and looking in on her old coworkers.

CHAPTER 12

THE PUKWUDGIES

The monsters of our imagination are often the smallest of things. They are cultivated in our bedrooms as children when we pull the sheets above our heads and peer over the top to make sure we are alone. We saw our toys through the dim glow of a nightlight and our daytime friends became shadows to be feared. Large monsters are intimidating, but they cannot fit under the bed or in the closet or in the corner of the room just beyond where the illumination hits. Small monsters can hide, sneak into thin cracks and slip out of sight.

Most cultures' mythology has some reference to little people and the mischief they can cause. The names and nature of the creatures change from culture to culture, but there are always common threads linking them together. Some are called monsters and roam the land looking for human food and kidnapping anyone they can find. Other are called demons, foul spirits feeding off the negative, exposing the sins of man. When referring to one, its classification gets blurred and these two words become interchangeable, perhaps showing us how closely associated these monsters are with evil.

The Wampanoag have their own version of the miniature demon know as the Pukwudgies or Puk-wudjees, and if most monsters are metaphors or symbols, the Pukwudgies separate themselves by their continued appearance in the forests and cemeteries of New England. Although between

An area near a Pukwudgie hunting ground. *Courtesy of Justin MyCofsky*

only two and three feet in height, they possess magic powers that make them more than just mischievous. They have been described as looking like small Native Americans or covered in thick hair from head to toe, and while the gap in their physical description may point to two different species of monsters, both have been known to haunt a stretch of land from Rhode Island to Cape Cod and eastern Massachusetts, through southern New Hampshire and into Maine.

While related very closely in physical appearance to the troll, they are said to employ darker and more powerful means to help them in their quest. They are accomplished magicians, conjuring magic sand that can blind their victim. Pukwudgies take the form of animals or insects and use their skills to confuse hunters or trap victims. They shoot poison arrows and spears, but can also attack with short knives. They can appear and disappear at will and some stories even give them the ability to fly.

The grander stories told of the monster are vintage mythology and a mixed bag of Wampanoag opinions on them. They were known to help humans or to ignore and avoid them. They did not get into the affairs of people unless they were stumbled upon. According to some legends, they became jealous of other mystical creatures who were nice to humans and felt left out and unwanted. They would then go out of their way to do the Wampanoag small favors, but their nature always got the better of them and they would turn back to their old ways.

Most stories about them focus on their darker side. It was easy to offend them and engage their anger, and they were known to fixate on one target or sweep entire villages away because of the offense of one member. They are often spoken of as pot-stirrers or instigators who used their magic to turn one person against another. They set the table and sit back while their enemies destroy themselves.

Their creation is unknown, but according to the book, *The Narrow Land* by Elizabeth Reynard, they are most often associated with one of the Wampanoag creation gods named Maushop. Like most polytheistic societies, the Wampanoag's gods tended to have more human qualities, and for all his power, Maushop lacked motivation and wisdom. The giant's missteps, often while trying to escape his wife or napping, are said to have created most of Cape Cod and the surrounding islands. The true thorns in his side were the Pukwudgies.

Maushop was often asked by his wife, Quant, to handle the mischievous monsters, but he ignored her. It was not until the first people on the earth, the early Wampanoags, asked him to help them that he finally put down his pipe and went after them. He would hunt the Pukwudgies down, shaking and confusing them once they were caught. He would toss them all around the land. Some would make their way back to Maushop, but more often than not, they would stay where they had landed.

Once, Maushop was away for a very long time, leaving his five sons and wife to handle the land and take care of the Pukwudgies. This coincides with the rise of the Wampanoag among the powerful tribes in New England. When he finally arrived back at home, he found his sons had failed in their jobs and the Pukwudgies had begun running wild. Their actions, seen before as foolish and playful, were now seen as evil by those who recorded the stories. If you believe the Pukwudgies to be only a legend, this might relate to some continued tragedy they suffered, such as the disease that took many of their numbers before the settlers arrived or the rise of the other tribes around them and the escalation of tensions with them. If the creatures are real, the question remains why they would chose to switch and become the enemy of the Wampanoag rather than just a nuisance.

The monsters were known to light fires, kidnap small children, and push people off rocks. Their hunting ground was near cliffs or running water, making an area like the Assonet Ledge in the forest an ideal spot and perhaps accounting for the various sightings of orbs, Native American ghosts, and the rash of unexplained suicides there. To complete their transformation to a more evil being, they began to lure hunters deeper into the woods and set upon them, sometimes in groups, and always taking no prisoners.

Maushop, being lazy and having been away from home for a while, was slow to start, but when he heard the monsters had taken his food and attacked his house, he sent his five sons after them. The Pukwudgies hid from the giants and then blinded them with magic sand and shot poisoned arrows at them until all five had fallen dead.

When Maushop and Quant heard of their sons' fall and deaths, they became enraged and hunted down as many of the demons as they could find. They squeezed the life out of them and stomped them into the ground, but there were too many. Some fled and scattered themselves throughout the known world. The remaining monsters quickly regrouped and set a trap for Maushop. They tricked him into the water and fired their arrows, wounding him and forcing him to retreat. Some tales say they killed him. Others say he ran away fearing another attack, and depressed over his sons, never returned to Massachusetts. Either way, the Pukwudgies claimed a victory over a creation god, a concept not found in the folklore of most cultures.

People who spend time in the forest will tell you Pukwudgies are not merely folklore. They continue to see them, and as the world develops around them, the monsters remain unchanged and as dark as ever. Today they seem to be seen by accident, but when someone stumbles upon them, they have a habit of making their presence known after the people leave the woods. They are slightly off the path in the forest, being observed by those who stray off the road, but they also haunt in the bedroom.

Joan was walking her dog through the forest on a cold Saturday morning in April when she saw the monster. Odd animals are not uncommon in a state forest where the land is often part of a reserve, but Joan knows what she saw was no animal. As she and her dog, Sid, walked down the path, Sid became anxious and strayed a few feet into the woods, something which he usually did not do. Joan followed him in, calling his name and whistling, but then stopped short. Her dog was lying completely flat in the leaves, and on a rock ten feet away was a Pukwudgie holding out his hand and looking at the dog.

She described him as looking like a troll; two feet high with pale gray skin and hair on his arms and the top of his head. The monster seemed to have no clothes, but it was difficult to tell because his stomach hung over his waist, almost touching his knees. His torso made up the majority of his body and he had very short legs. His eyes were a deep green, and he had large lips and a long, almost canine nose. She is not sure how she knew, but the creature felt masculine to her.

The Pukwudgie turned his attention to Joan and stood watching her, staring straight at her with no expression, almost like it was stunned to see her. She froze and remembers thinking the air in her lungs had been pushed out.

"It stood there and just watched me. It was like he was sizing me up, trying to decide what

The spot of Joan's sighting.

to do." Sid finally came to and ran back towards the trail, dragging Joan who was still holding the leash tightly. After gaining control of the dog, Joan decided it was best to leave the forest. "I didn't go back to see if it was still there. I knew it was. It wasn't scared of me and didn't look like it was going to run away."

Although the whole exchange took less than thirty seconds, it remains with Joan ten years later. She has not gone back to the forest, but feels that might not be enough. Three times since the event, she has woken up to find the demon looking in on her. It has never attacked or spoken to her. She has merely seen it looking through her bedroom window where it stays just long enough for her to notice. All three times she claims she was fully awake and could have moved, if she had to.

"Seeing it in the forest scared me. But seeing it in the window at night, staring like it knew me, made me move."

Joan now lives in a town in a different county, but her fear is echoed by other people who have seen the beast. Tom's two encounters with the Pukwudgies have not discouraged his trips to the forest. The forest takes on a different personality in the dark, and Tom would often sneak into the woods in his late teens to sort things out. While he admits he was in a depressed state when he saw the monster, he becomes very serious when discussing how genuine his sighting was. He claims he was not under the influence of drugs or alcohol, and was not so emotionally upset that it clouded his judgment.

The first time he saw them he had snuck out of the house and made the mile walk to one of the entrances. He began down one of the paths, playing an especially bad day over and over in his mind. The moon was close to full and had lit his way during his trip to the forest, but like many reports, he says there was almost no moonlight that made its way into the woods. He noticed movement about ten feet in front of him and stopped.

"I noticed a dim light, like in the form of a ball, in front of me. It was white and swelled, like it was breathing. I was completely entranced by it (in a later interview, Tom clarified he meant he was interested in the light and not hypnotized). It rose to about my shoulders and then flew into the trees."

Tom followed the light into the woods, only to find it had gone. He walked back to the path, confused, but when he pushed the branches aside, he could not find the path that had been there moments before. He began to get nervous that he had become lost in the forest, until he saw the light again. Not knowing exactly why, he followed it. When he was three feet away, it disappeared and he found himself back where he had started.

"It was impossible. I didn't even walk the same way, but somehow I was in the exact same place." He turned to start back home, when he noticed a small man about two and a half feet tall with fur all over his body. The only facial feature he could make out was his nose, which Tom said looked long, "like a werewolf's." The Pukwudgie moaned and ran into the woods.

Tom reports what he saw had walked upright and had used its arms to push something aside when he fled to the woods. He had moved with a slight limp, but "like a human."

The second time Tom saw the Pukwudgies, he had pulled his car into the parking lot on Copicut Road. He turned off the lights and lowered the radio to almost a whisper. He was singing to himself, turning his head side to side to try and detect any police, when he saw the same figure he had seen on the path. This time it was staring at him from twenty feet in front of the car. Tom again noticed the large nose, but was more taken by the Pukwudgies glowing red eyes. The car turned on by itself and his radio began to get louder. He pulled out of the parking lot and took the long way home to try and stop his hands from shaking.

Although the experiences were two years apart, Tom feels he saw the same creature both times and the creature had recognized him. "He wanted me to leave, so I did."

Tom was hesitant to share what he had experienced, but he started to hear stories from other people about them. "Anyone who spends enough time in there sees them. People don't talk about it too much, but if they come up, everyone has a story."

For their size, the Pukwudgies have great power that the Wampanoag saw as magic. One of their most valuable magical powers was to train and control the Tei-Pai-Wankas, which in Native American legend is a burst of energy in the form of a light that acted like a wild animal or, in some tales, a wild human. The Pukwudgies used these lights to attract the attention of hunters and lead them into the woods. Tom's experience in the forest echoes the connection between these two supernatural forces.

American and European folklorist and paranormal investigators know these lights well and have long associated them with their research. In folklore, they are referred to as Will-o-the-Wisps and are thought to be the souls of the departed. Investigators call them orbs, and they are the gold standard of proof of the supernatural. They scan pictures searching for them and seeing them in the field is enough to make the night worth while.

The Freetown Forest, like many areas in Bristol County, has a long history of these lights. People have reported seeing them in the sky above the forest, and ufologists consider them proof of UFOs or alien contact. Orbs have also been associated with the souls of Natives Americans who have died in the area. In nearby Rehoboth, Massachusetts, there are several reports of people who have seen these lights at locations of battles occurring during King Phillip's War, and the lights are accompanied by disembodied voices talking in what people believe to be Native American languages. In the forest itself, these lights have been seen while native chanting has been heard.

The nature of the Tei-Pai-Wankas is unclear, allowing questions to arise. Are these balls of light the souls of Wampanoags somehow trapped on this Earth, so confused and directionless that the Pukwudgies can take advantage of them? Are they still trying to trap their old prey, even in death? Is that the reason there are so many lights connected with the voices of the dead within the trees?

Regardless of the answer, Tei-Pai-Wankas and their dark masters have been tormenting people in the woods for centuries.

In 1982, Jean Fritz published the children book, *The Good Giants and the Bad Pukwudgies*, preserving the lore of the monster for small children and folklorists alike. In the book, the reader sees a kinder version of the monster, but even a title for children could not hide their evil nature. In pictures more likely to inspire nightmare than imaginations, the little men are seen burning huts and kidnapping small children, but the book moved a lost myth off of a dusty shelf into the minds of paranormal investigators.

People in the woods do not have to read the stories. Although none have ever reporting being attacked, the fear they felt was something more vivid than any legend alone could inspire. For them, the experience is not for children to hear, but a warning that something is not right in the forest.

CHAPTER 13

THE WITCH OF THE WOODS

The foundation of the witch's house.

Investigating the paranormal is not always a straight line. There are times when the pieces do not fall neatly into place and the picture is more clouded than when you began. It can become frustrating, but if you take a step back, you see the story as proof of the interconnectedness of the paranormal and see the questions as a sign that you should never think you have everything worked out.

Dave's experiences involve several kinds of hauntings in the same location, and his story becomes a mixed bag of religion and legend, and just when there is enough confusion to make an investigator's head spin, there is still the actual haunting to deal with. Dave is a firm believer in the paranormal, although he does not seek out ghosts and does not watch television shows about the subject. His interest is only in trying to make sense of what happened to him and in finding someone to believe him. "A lot of people get excited when I tell them what happened. They want it to happen to them. At this point in my life, I never want anything like that to happen to me again."

Even though the experience is now behind him, he still deals with it, waking up some nights wondering if he will see the white-haired lady again.

Behind Profile Rock there is a vast cranberry bog stretching over acres. Surrounding the bog are thin woods which lead to the backyards of residential homes. This is where Dave grew up, on an average street in a rural town surrounded by forests and cranberries. There was something else in the neighborhood, however, which made itself known to the young males, haunting their dreams and revealing just enough to keep them on their toes.

The paranormal is often defined by the people who experience it, and Dave believes the boys in his neighborhood were haunted by a witch. All of the boys had seen her in their dreams, but in the waking hours, she took many forms, leading to a darker and older explanation for the story they found themselves in. Dave and his friends were being stalked by a demon.

"It's kind of like a legend in the neighborhood I grew up in," says Dave. "Well, more the boys. Strangely, none of this stuff ever happened to girls. As we got older we started talking about it and realized it was happening to all of us. We all agreed that was where it was coming from."

The being first made itself known to Dave while he was still very young. He was six and playing in his backyard when he heard a loud and scary laughing from the woods a few feet away. "We started hearing someone laughing out in the woods, says Dave today, remembering how he and his friend were scared, but also curious as to what was making the noise." When they looked to where the noise was coming from, they saw a figure hidden among the trees. He could not make out any features. In fact, he could not see anything at all. Instead, Dave found himself looking straight at a perfectly camouflaged person, the light refracted all around it so it formed nothing more than a distortion of the environment around it. "It was just moving along in the woods. And there was the weird, sick laugh." If you did not know to look, you would have missed it, but it was clearly there. He and his friend ran into the house and never told anyone what they had seen.

The experience would have been forgotten if the haunting hadn't continued. At the age of ten, he saw the witch for the first time, although it was in a dream. Behind his woods there was a trail leading out to the edge of the bog and a small pond. He had never made it out that far before, but in his dream he knew just where to go. Armed with an ax for reasons he never understood, he made his way back to a small house on the edge of the pond. Feeling the kind of courage you only have in dreams, he entered.

"As I walked in, I saw a woman in bed with an Indian. I ended up killing them both. It was a really strange thing." In the dream, Dave was an adult and he remembers thinking the witch was somehow cheating on him. He does not understand why he killed the couple, even given his jealousy, but he woke up in a cold sweat.

Dave describes the woman as a witch, mainly due to her appearance. She was dressed in a long black robe that just about touched the ground. She had wild gray hair, but she did not appear to be old. She did not have deep lines or wrinkles on her face, but instead appeared middle aged. Her eyes were brown and larger than a normal person's. To this day, the most telling feature of the woman for Dave is still her wild hair and the evil look she gave him.

This seemed to have triggered a rise in the activity. A few years later, he and some friends were walking in the woods when things became vaguely familiar to Dave and he started to lead the way. They eventually came across the foundation of an old house. There were two rooms to the old stone structure with a small set of stairs. Off to the side was a well. Dave immediately recognized it as the foundation from the house he had seen in his dream.

It was at this point the boys began to compare notes. They had all seen the woman Dave described. She usually appeared outside their windows, asking to be let in. They all said they had a hard time remembering if they were asleep or awake when it happened, but they all felt she was evil and never invited her in.

The odd distortion in the woods continued as well. Dave saw it several more times entering into his mid-teens, and always felt it was the witch staring at him. Sometimes he saw it while walking or riding his bike on the trail, or while fishing in the small reservoir near the bog. The sightings were almost always connected with the insane laughing and his reaction was always to remove himself from the situation. He began to see the laughing as a warning sign, but other times he would feel like something was wrong and he needed to leave, only to start hearing the voice.

He saw the witch several more times over the next few years, always in his dreams. One of the most disturbing ones occurred when he was fourteen. "I was out in the cranberry bogs with two of the neighborhood kids I was friends with back then. We decided to head back to the house. When I got to the main path I look up. The witch was at the top of the rise and she was slowly floating down the path towards us." He yelled to his friends and ran through the woods to his house. He looked back and the woods parted, revealing the witch killing the two small boys with something in her hand. She threw the object at him, but he woke up before it hit him.

"I woke up in bed in a cold sweat, breathing hard. I was awake. I turned to look towards my window and she was floating outside my window." She asked Dave if she could come in and he screamed and ran into his living room. When he went back a few minutes later, she was done.

One friend of his allowed the witch in and the decision became such a disturbance his family was forced to leave the neighborhood. "He had a dream one night where she came to his window and he let her in." She forced the boy to have sex with her, causing the friend to scream. When the parent came running to help, they were unable to open the door and were forced to break it down to get to their son. "They found him in there naked like he was being held down. When they woke him up he was incoherent and started screaming about some witch coming in through the window."

In total, at least five boys in the neighborhood experienced the dreams or had encounters with the same kind of unexplained activity Dave reports. Despite the feeling of being stalked by the witch, the boys in the neighborhood made several visits to the foundation, and Dave admits he traveled back there at least twenty times himself.

The road where Jeremy saw the witch and the figures in the woods.

Things rarely happened, or they were not shared, but they were all seeking some kind of reason for seeing what they were seeing.

One friend in particular became obsessed with seeing the woman. Dave would take him around the trails, trying to make contact with whatever it was in the woods. As usually happens, when they least expected it, the ghost found them.

"We were walking around the trail. I don't even think we were looking for anything that day. As we were walking through the woods, I was in front of him. I felt him stop. I turned back and saw him looking off into the woods." About thirty feet away from them was a stalk white figure in the shape of a person, about six feet in height running through the woods. After confirming they both saw the same thing, they decided to quickly leave the woods.

After they had taken a few moments to calm down and process what they had seen, their courage came back. They agreed to go back to see if they could get a better look at what they had seen. They were unable to find anything, but decided to walk a bit further down the path, moving closer to the Witch's House. From the tree in front of them they began to hear the same eerie laughter Dave always associated with the Witch. About twenty yards off into the woods was the distorted apparition standing next to a tree.

"That's where the laughter was coming from." Scared, they ran to leave. According to Dave's friend, something pushed him from behind causing him to fall and trip Dave. The laughter was now all around them and, as they ran through the woods, they could hear branches crashing to the ground behind them. When they got to the front of the house, a black cat was sitting on top of Dave's car, waiting for them. It looked at them as they approached, jumped down, and ran into the woods.

When you consider what they had just experienced, the appearance of a cat should not have scared the two, but the cat was well known to Dave, and even though he knows it might be the hardest aspect of his story to believe, he has seen the cat act more human than animal.

The first time he was not prepared for its behavior. He had just gotten his driver's license and decided to visit his friend up the street. The cat was in the middle of the road and refused to move when he hit the horn. He drove around it, but when he looked in his rearview mirror he saw something that sent his heart into his throat. "It walked off on two legs into the woods."

He saw it move on two legs again a short time later. He was with some friends at the Witch's House and it was sitting on the foundation. As they approached, it jumped down on two legs, turned around to give them one last look and ran into the woods, the whole time remaining on only its hind legs.

The cat seems an unusual addition to the ghosts in the area, but there might be a connection. "I don't know if it ties in with anything, it is just something we always associated with her." It has been seen twice in relation to specific hauntings. In addition, there was no one in the neighborhood who owned such a cat, and it was not seen all the time, reducing the chance it was a stray or just lost and living in the woods.

The black cat is a common figure in the world of the paranormal. Often witches who had made deals with the Devil for their power were said to own the animals, using them as spies, messengers, and protectors. They were called familiars and many of our superstitions related to the dark animal spring from the belief that they signaled a witch nearby. Another aspect of the legend involves the cat being the witch herself. Many were thought to have the ability to transform into an animal and roam the night. There are tales of harming such animals only to find an injury to the suspected witch in the same area of the body the next day.

Looking back, Dave and his friends realized the sightings and attacks always happened between mid-September and late October. "It was every year something was happening to me. It got so I would start to dread September and October rolling around." This time period coincides with increased cult activity in the forest and an important time frame in the Satanic Calendar, ending with Halloween. One person in the neighborhood who was a few years older than Dave was active in a small group of teens who practiced their own kind of devil worship. They would use the foundation as a meeting place, and during the fall, would camp out and perform their rituals in the old house.

More than ten years have passed since Dave experienced anything in the woods, but what happened during those years has never been settled to him. He often goes back to his parents' house and will take his girlfriend's son on the path. Although he is half a mile from the Witch's House, he still feels uneasy even being on it and leaves quickly.

Recently, he decided to go back, and even with so much time passed since the last occurrence, his stomach became tighter as he approached. The area was very different. Some of the foundation had been knocked down and there were truck tracks and boundary markers all around. The well and retaining wall was still there, but now he noticed several other areas blocked off with old-fashioned stone walls. There is something odd in the way the properties are sectioned off, however. While most New England stone walls block off large areas, marking acres of land settled centuries ago, these partition off plots of only several hundred feet with distinct corners, creating a pattern which implies a close community living tightly together.

The Freetown Historical Society reports no known settlements in that area during colonial times or in more recent days. The reason for the walls, much like the hauntings the boys of the neighborhood experienced, remains lost. Dave still looks for answers to the odd woman who preoccupied so much of his youth, but he is unsure if he will go back to the foundation. Although he was much braver and explored parts of the woods he had never looked at when he was younger, he could not shake the feelings he was having. He was all too eager to return to the thorn bushes and to walk over the washed out paths to get back to his parent's house.

"I still have that feeling. Any time I expected to see something again." He has lost touch with the other boys he used to play with, and he assumes they have not had any other experiences as well. With the added development of the land, and with new houses being built and the neighborhood expanding, a new generation of boys will begin playing among the trees. If the witch still walks the woods, she might have all the company she ever needs.

CHAPTER 14

CRYSTAL SPRINGS

Many haunted locations stay off the map for years. People experience ghosts when they are alone or isolated, and question whether anything ever happened. If they come to terms with what they experienced, they still find it hard to share for fear of being laughed at. When the haunted building houses a high number of people, it eventually gets out. Once one person shares their story, others come forward, and the ghost stories become the subject of everyday socializing. Everyone has a story.

Crystal Springs, outside the forest but in keeping with the haunted traditions of the town is one of those places. It is another of the haunted schools in Massachusetts that seem to attract spirits. Today the school is run by the Institute for Developmental Disabilities, Incorporated and serves males and females with behavior and healthcare issues stemming from cognitive impairment. It offers individual and group therapy to its clients, but over the past few years there have started to be reports of other inhabitants who make the building their home.

According to former employees, the Brayden building was the first of the dorms to be built, but over the years Crystal Springs has expanded, and as the land has evolved, so has the clientele. This makes finding the origins of the spirits difficult, but offers a possible key to what might be haunting the employees.

Like many of the haunted schools in the area, there does not seem to be just one type of ghost experienced by the patients and staff. The most common occurrences are phantom voices, sometimes heard several times in one night or once over a series of nights. The voice is reported to be female, but no one can say how old she is or even if it is the same woman each time. Different people hear the voice differently, but it never seems threatening or even sad.

"I could handle the voices, but it's the knocking that used to get to me," claims Valerie, a former employee who worked in several of the buildings over her time there. "I know that sounds crazy, but I got used to hearing my name. When those knocks would happen, it scared me." Valerie reports the knocking would take on a personality, almost as if she could tell the emotional state of the spirit by how it knocked. "Sometimes we would hear a loud bang instead, like someone threw a piece of equipment on the floor. Those were the nights you thought twice about going out for a cigarette."

Crystal Springs is also known for it ghosts showing their emotions through lights. While working long night shifts, employees can easily dismiss when they see a light turn on in a room they just left and locked. It is so common, some reported not even noticing anymore. It is harder to ignore when they see the lights flicker for no reason or have them turn off when they enter an isolated room. This kind of haunting happens less frequently, but is always more disturbing.

Seeing figures move in the hallways has also become part of the nightly rituals of the employees. The figure, seen as solid by some and as nothing more than a shadow or fog by others, moves from one dark area to another, always just out of view. When staff check, there is nothing there, and sometimes the hall becomes extremely cold. This is the most intimidating ghost for those who experience it because it seems to be toying with them.

Joy worked at the day shift for several years, but would sometimes be asked to cover at night. She was always hesitant because she is a self described, "scaredy cat." "It wanted us to know it was there. It was a man too, or it felt like a man. He wanted us to see him but not get a good look. Just enough so we knew he was there." This figure has been seen at other schools, asylums, and hospitals, almost as if he is feeding off the negative energy alive in those places.

Although she had lived most of her life with the paranormal, Darlene was not sure about the haunting at Crystal Springs. She had often seen unexplained things in her house in Freetown long before she ever went to work there. She had experienced people walking in and out of her room and had seen the ghosts of possible residents who had lived in the house her father had torn down to build over circling her bed. She began working at the school in the late eighties and heard the rumors of ghosts almost upon starting. "When I first came, everyone said, 'Be careful. Weird things go on. Lights shut off and on when they're not supposed to. You hear noises, and when you go to check, there is nothing there. You see things move down the hallway.' I thought, 'Sure. Okay. What are you on?'"

She spent over a year there, and says she experienced exactly what they had described at night. As a child, some of the ghosts visiting her were so scary she would wake up her parents screaming, but nothing she saw or heard at Crystal Springs ever felt that intense. She does remember feeling unsettled, mainly because she considers herself psychically sensitive and was always afraid they would try and contact her.

"Sometimes you would feel this cold on the back of your neck and the hairs would stand up." She grew to learn the cold spots she felt usually meant something would happen soon. She wishes now she had tracked when the ghosts would make themselves known. She feels there was a pattern. Hauntings would happen in cycles, maybe once a night for a period of time and then stopping for long stretches. For Darlene and others who worked there, the lull was worse, the time just waiting for the next knock or whisper.

Darlene mostly experienced the voices. "I thought I would hear them call my name," Darlene describes, laughing now at the entire situation. She would respond, "but there would be nobody there." This happened to her more than once, and its frequency, along with the stories she had heard, convinced her there was something there. The voice usually came from down a hallway she was in, regardless of where she was in the building. She always thought it might be a client or another staff member, but there was never a place for the person to hide or escape. Darlene says now she believes the voice was a female, but she is not sure if this is because she assumed it was a woman because all of the staff was female or because of the familiar tone the voice took.

"I'd call out and nothing. Then I'd call out again and I'd hear, 'Ya,' from the girl I was working with." Darlene says the voice of her coworker would come from a different direction, so she knew it was not the original one she had heard.

Darlene would also have other bizarre things happen to her. Although they are not as definitive as the voices, she feels they still remain unexplained. "Sometimes we would see the lights go off and on, or we would turn a light off and come back and it was on." For the people she worked with it became a sort of joke, but they always remembered which lights were on and which were off so they could tell something had happened.

Like many hauntings, the subtle moments are the ones to be feared. They are the times when you know something is not right, but there is not enough evidence, or the episode is not dramatic enough to share or tell people about. "Many times I would get the feeling there was something behind me. I would turn around, but there would be no one there." For her, this was the worst kind of incident because she could not tell if whatever she had felt was trying to scare her or whether she had just picked up on something passing by. Intent makes all the difference.

Now that she is gone, and thinking about it almost two decades removed, she feels the ghosts are not there to scare people, and nothing ever happened to make her so afraid she did not want to return. "Sometimes we would be together and something would happen." This was usually a loud banging or something moving down the furthest end, just out of the light. "One of us would get the nerve to go down there, and by the time we did, there was nothing there."

Mariana has had family members and friends work at Crystal Springs over the years and spent a year there herself as a nurse. She often heard knocking and would respond but find no one. She admits to having been scared many nights she worked there, and when the administration was not around, most of the staff would whisper about what they had seen. Unlike some other haunted buildings, the experienced employees shared their stories with the newbies before they'd have something happen to them. It could be that the warning sets the tone and almost guarantees the new people will have something happen. Many of the hauntings happen when the women are alone, which sometimes makes them feel like it never happened. Sharing the stories becomes one of the only ways to prove anything had happened at all and also a way to form a bond with others who have experienced it.

Mariana shares her stories almost like they are campfire tales. "A nurse once told me the story of a young man she saw walk right through a wall in the infirmary, which is always locked and you need to be buzzed in to gain entry. She said he walked past her and just went right through the wall." This kind of story is shared often, but the ghost doing the walking is not always the same. At times it is an old woman. It is also seen as a ball of light. Other times, it is a small child or a teenage boy about the age of a resident.

Carol, who worked the nightshift, also saw an old woman once while filling out a crossword puzzle late one night. "She walked right by me. She didn't turn or even acknowledge I was there. I don't think I *was* there to her. She just walked past, but when I leaned over to ask her who she was, I saw she was floating a few inches above the ground. Her feet were moving, but she was float-ing." The elderly woman passed right through the door, but Carol was too frightened to follow her and see where she went.

She describes the woman as being in her late seventies or early eighties and dressed in a white gown with a blue sweater. The woman appeared completely solid until the moment she went through the door and Carol remembers expecting her to hurt herself as she hit it. She also noticed the woman had a distressed look on her face, "like something was wrong or she was looking for something important." Although she did not notice it at the time, when directly asked, she remembered the room getting very warm right before she saw her.

There is no direct evidence to prove who the woman might be. There have been old woman who have died over the years dating back to its days as a hospital, but there is nothing about her description or manner suggesting why her spirit might have remained there. The residence she was seen in is rumored to be one of the oldest houses in Freetown, recently moved and updated.

One ghost who might be able to be tracked down is the young man seen by several staff members wearing a leather jacket. He is described as having short, sandy hair, becoming long in the back. In addition to the jacket, he is reported wearing blue jeans. He is usually seen in an area known as the Tree Houses because they were created a few years ago from a wooded area within the property.

According to Mariana, a nurse told her she had seen the man a few times, always in the same place. She had also seen him on the grounds one night. The nurse was returning from delivering the evening medicines to the patients when she heard a car noise from the outside. "She then said that she had her car and wasn't getting a ride.

When the nurse looked out the window she saw the man who had walked through the wall a few weeks before standing against a pole."

It is rumored there was an automobile accident near the property a few years before the incident. Two sets of teens were drag racing when one lost control and died. The description of the dead man, known by many residents of Freetown, matched the ghost, and he was always known to wear a brown leather bomber jacket.

Some of the ghosts seen at Crystal Springs might be the souls of a family buried on the property. Behind the infirmary is a small graveyard with the name "Evans" on many of the tombstones. Many of the dates are too worn out by time to be read. No one seems to remember exactly who the family is, but staff avoid it. Those who have gone out to it have seen flashes of light and felt as if they were being watched. One reported seeing a small girl walking near there who then ducked down and disappeared. Most report an eerie and uneasy feeling in their stomach when they enter.

There are other unexplained things happening at Crystal Springs. Although not entirely paranormal, there are also reports of the clients moving through the building at odd speeds, or appearing in places very quickly and without a good explanation as to how they got there. There is never anything said by the people, but the staff even went so far as to search for a secret passage they might be traveling though. This is still unexplained and has been reported by several staff members.

No formal paranormal investigation has ever occurred at the school, and the foundation of the stories, as well as any possible reason for the hauntings, cannot be proven. Perhaps the passing of older clients in the original building has left behind some part of the past. Maybe the more recent developing has disturbed something which is now awake and taking form for people to see.

Perhaps there is even a scientific explanation. Recently, investigators and parapsychologist have questioned mental health disorders and disorders of the brain and have begun to connect it with supernatural experiences. Although only theoretical, some believe troubles with the brain, such as epilepsy or MS, might make a person more likely to experience ghosts because the part of the brain filtering out those experiences is damaged.

At Crystal Springs, all of these factors, mixed with late lonely nights, cause bumps in the night.

In a town where reports of cults and ghosts and monsters can be found around every corner, the activity at Crystal Springs might seem tame by comparison. Voices in the dark might not be able to compare to phantom fires, but the employees know the unknown. It is as much a part of their night as dolling out medication. They pass the time hoping nothing happens and passing stories along when they do. If all of the hauntings were to end tomorrow, ghosts in the halls and the dark man moving from corner to corner would remain, and that might be enough to get through the shift.

CHAPTER 15

BLACK MAGIC AND SATANISTS IN THE SOUTHEAST

Massachusetts has a long relationship with the Devil. Shortly after the King Philip's War, the Salem Witch trials broke out in present day Danvers, Massachusetts. In those days the small community saw no difference between witchcraft and Satan, but rather defined witches by their re-

Courtesy of Big Operation Productions

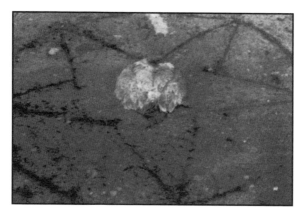

More evidence found in the woods.
Courtesy of Big Operations Productions

lationship to the Devil. When one was accused of being a witch it meant they had made a pact with him and their offenses became crimes against the people and against God.

Modern witches, be they Wiccan or another form of neo-paganism, have little relation to their ancestors from Salem. Most do not believe in the Devil at all, but rather have a strong connection to nature or the natural forces around them. They use these forces to try and effect their environment or strife to strengthen their relationship to the larger picture. They are attracted to places of high energy and often find themselves drawn to places within Freetown, specifically the State Forest, for reasons they cannot explain.

Their activity is rarely criminal, usually being no more serious than trespassing, and their places of worship are often mistaken for the darker elements within the woods. They are important to address because they feel the energy in the forest and use it in a religious way, much the same way the Wampanoag feel the sacredness of the land.

Satanists and witches who deal with the dark side of witchcraft tend to find the same places within the forest, causing many to confuse the groups and condemn the innocent and misunderstood. Often their symbols overlap and cause confusion, feeding the distrust the majority has to neo-pagans. The important thing about all of these groups, Satanist, magician, or dark magician, is they see the forest as a source of energy, and their activity helps to cycle the forces there. The second thing to remember is all are protected by the Constitution and have the right to believe and practice as long as it does not violate laws.

If you look at where these groups are centered, Cape Cod, Central Massachusetts, Freetown, Taunton, you see high levels of paranormal activities in the same places. Most of these groups meet in wooded areas or secluded buildings, and when you step back, you also see a higher level of reports of ghosts. Those areas are also flooded by odd animals and alien abductions. This tends to create a connection between the two, although it is difficult to say who attracts who.

Practitioners seek out these places, perhaps knowing something we do not. Cycles of energy suck other elements in to encourage and take energy from, keeping what might be working in the forest alive. Most religions that work on the idea of using the energy found in nature will tell you there are some places that have more than others. Their activity might also bring energy in, creating a safe place for the supernatural to settle, or by generating energy, the paranormal can use it to manifest.

In recent years, Satanic cults have gained attention in Massachusetts. In 1988, there seemed to be a tide of activity, although no one knows for sure if the groups were related to each other or the significance of the time. None of these groups were connected to or had any known relationship to established Satanic groups, but worked on similar ideas and used the more established religions, such as the Church of Satan, as inspiration.

In Revere, Massachusetts, there were several animals killed, beheaded, and left on the beach, including a lamb, several chickens, and a rooster. In Cambridge a few weeks later, more dead roosters were found. The Wompatuck State Park in Hingham, Massachusetts, experienced its own version of cult fever in 1988. There were reports of an active cult using a munitions bunker there to hold ceremonies. Although they were believed to be harmless and practicing a form of witchcraft mixed with ideas based on role-playing games, other investigators found more disturbing elements to their trespassing, including Satanic tattoos, animal bones on alters, and ritual weapons. A similar cult was spotted in the same location for the next ten years, always right out of the reach of law enforcement.

In the same year, Satan was busy on the other side of Boston. The actions of a cult in Lynn were deemed a public nuisance, and a mansion where they held their rituals was forced to be torn down to stop them. Essex law enforcement began bringing in experts to speak because the problem was so bad in towns like Gloucester, Wenham, and Rockport. In those towns, they found a close link between drug trafficking and the occult.

Most believed these reports of black masses and vandalism to be nothing more than kids fooling around and experimenting. Reports were generally kept out of the news and died quickly when they made it to the papers. This is typical, according to Detective Alan Alves. "Everyone wants it to not get out. Police don't want to give other people ideas and the businesses and real estate people don't want the property values to go down. No one likes it, so [an investigation] just stalls."

Although many believe it predates the practices of groups in other locations in Massachusetts, Freetown was slow to gain attention. The Devil is alive in the Freetown State Forest. People can debate religion or the nature of the dark spirits living there, but those who follow Satan and his minions have a history there. There is a darker side to witchcraft. Many will say there is no white or black magic, but rather intention. There are some groups in Massachusetts whose intentions are nothing but evil. They practice the negative side of witchcraft or become involved in Voodoo, Palo Mayombe, or Satanism. They sense the same spots other neo-paganists do, and these spots become magnets for people tapped into negative forces. They, in fact, may be more attracted to places like the forest because of the forces at work there.

Satanism and Satanists live in the shadows of our society, but if you pay attention and you know what to look for, their signs are everywhere. The past fifty years, maybe longer, have been spent tricking our eyes, making the symbols of the most dangerous cult commonplace to us. Instead of the traditional image, we are given an accessible character presented in human form which attracts and repels us at the same time. Symbols of occultism are now more fashionable. Once adopted by antisocial and nonconformist groups, the images have become mainstream, diluting their power and changing people's opinions on what they mean. Many are now used by popular music or even clothing companies until our exposure to them washes over us and goes unnoticed. It is not just the imagery in heavy metal music or fringe clothing, but rather a slow incorporating into the more widely accepted markets.

The majority of Satanists who find their way to Freetown are dabblers. They have certain feelings of isolation and Satanism offers them the opportunity to connect to a group. These small groups meet and practice some form of ceremony, usually using the more organized and public groups, such as the Anton LaVey's Church of Satan, as their model and mixing their beliefs with others brought in from literature, like *The Satanic Bible*, music, and pop culture. These groups are not criminal by nature, usually only resorting to drug use, graffiti, and trespassing. However, they can become dangerous. Some have been known to get caught up in the life and graduate to animal cruelty, sacrifice, and even homicide.

These group's calling cards have been seen throughout the forest, at times out in the open and obvious and other times hidden between the lines. Their graffiti, often mistaken for innocent writing, litters areas such as the Ledge and Profile Rock. An excellent example is a piece of graffiti found at the Ledge in the Freetown Forest. Written in white against the rock was a name and what seemed a class year. Underneath was an upside down cross and then the letters "BOC." At first glance, this seems to be no more than a person marking his name, graduation year, and his favorite band, Blue Oyster Cult. The markings, however, could mean more.

Martin, a member of a Satanic cult in the mid-nineties explains the relationship when he sees the picture. First, the person's name is underlined and the underlining blends into the symbols, a clear sign there is a stronger connection between the two than just a band and a fan. The name is written slightly off center, which Martin takes to mean either a leaning to the left, often associated with Satanic activity, or off center enough just to tell people to pay attention.

Often, a cult member will want to associate itself with a band because its symbols mean some-

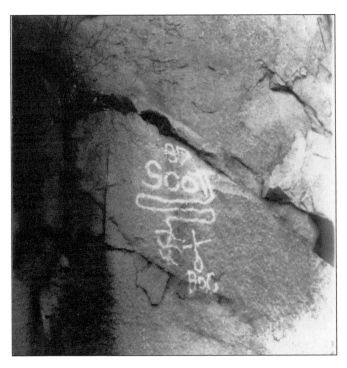

Band graffiti linked to possible Satanic activity.

thing to them. The band itself might have a connection to the occult, but the group takes those symbols and incorporates them into their belief system. Harmless markings now become the hidden symbols of the group. Only the initiated truly understand the meaning, and it becomes a way to feel part of the something.

For example, one former cult member in Freetown was part of a group who worshiped Alster Crowley, one of the most powerful men cults to attach themselves to. His group incorporated symbols of the god Apollo into their ceremonies, not because Crowley talked about Apollo, but because Led Zeppelin often spoke of him and one of their symbols was Apollo. This group also was rumored to be heavily into the occult and was linked to

Crowly. This secondary connection galvanized the group and acted as an inspiration for ceremonies.

The activity of these groups is not just limited to writing on rocks. Throughout the eighties and nineties, police discovered evidence of animal abuse throughout the forest. Pentagrams were found with dead birds in the middle. Extinguished fires were found with animal bones, often those of small animals such as squirrels, around them. Other times pentagrams were found made of stone with blood on the rocks and in the middle. Although no tests were done on the evidence, it was presumed to be the blood of members and animal sacrifices.

Some of the smaller cases throughout Freetown have helped to paint the reputation of the town, and in some cases, have sparked a mythology all their own. In late 1991, a teenager cut his leg and wrote the Our Father backwards and upside down on a small piece of poster board in his own blood. He walked to St. Bernard Church on Main Street and removed the Baby Jesus. In its place he left a pile of bones and spilled more blood on the statue before he left.

In 1990, a grave was dug up from a cemetery deep within the forest. It was the second time in a year the grave had been hit, and no one is sure why Elizabeth Gregory, who died in 1868, would be the target of attack. Her body had been removed by someone in 1989, and it is believed the same people had come back the next year looking for something left in the grave. The body and the people responsible for removing her have never been found. There might be a connection between her disappearance and the sighting of zombies in the forest. Perhaps the dead was raised and she returned to her own grave for some reason a year later. Of course, most in law enforcement are more comfortable passing the incidents off as the actions of a youth cult.

Perhaps the most famous case of small cult crime took place in 1991, perhaps inspired by the actions in 1989 and 1990. Four teens drove out to the Assonet Burying Ground, just outside the forest. Two entered the Robert Wyatt Mausoleum and removed the head of Angie Littlefield. They ran back to the car with only the head, but the other two teens, who did not believe the others would go through with it, forced them to toss the head out the window. The head was eventually recovered and the two youths were charged with several crimes, including breaking and entering at night and disinterring remains.

Since the incident, the headless woman has become the source of legend. Some have said the group was Satanist and intended to use the head in ceremonies. "They use the head to drink from," says Detective Alan Alves. "It's a source of power for some groups. You drink from the person's head and you gain more energy." Others have said the group was just bored and looking for trouble, and the disinterment was only part of a prank. The truth is probably somewhere in the middle, but evil has a way of moving the pieces for its own good.

The date of Ms. Littlefield's death, April 22, 1914, coincides with major cult activity through-out the country. Besides a heightened level of abductions and odd murders, there is a connec-tion between major events of wickedness during this time in April. Hitler was born on April 20th and the events of Waco, Texas, and the Oklahoma

City bombing both happened on April 19th. The Columbine Massacre occurred on the 20th, although it was originally planned for the day before. While it can be said each event inspired the others (Timothy McVeigh has said he bombed the Federal Building in honor of the events of Waco), there might be a deeper conspiracy manipulating things to happen during the build up to Da Maer or the Grand Climax on the Satanic calendar. The days before the ritual are known as a time to cause chaos and gather victims for sacrifice. Satanic cults have long been known to use the same symbols as Hitler. The Nazis were thought to be heavily into the occult and might have practiced a form of Satanism.

If this was the only activity in Freetown, it might have been passed off as kids being kids. Although illegal, no task force is ever formed for scattered animal bones and grave robbing. Instead, larger, more organized groups, were discovered using the forest. Although the true nature of these groups remains a mystery to some degree and can only be theorized about, their crimes were much more severe. Instead of squirrels and birds, this group graduated to cows and possibly humans.

Alan Alves, Cult Detective

In 1996, the town of Freetown awarded one of its police officers a settlement of $345,000, the result of a case brought before the Massachusetts Commission Against Discrimination by a Cape Verdean lieutenant who had been part of the town his whole life and had served it for the past twenty-five years. To many in the town, the policeman had become a thorn in the side of town politics for years, but other knew him as a hard but fair man who worked to clear all of the cases he came across. Although the size of the settlement might raise some eyebrows, the politics reflect the same scene played out all over America. In any other town, the officer might have been nothing more than a simple civil servant who spent the majority of his days rescuing cats and clocking speeders.

In Freetown, the local policeman became a nationally recognized authority on the occult. His resume reads like a list of pulp fiction novels, and even if no one can agree on his motives or character, he is the heart of some of the worst crimes to hit Massachusetts over the past thirty years. Alan Alves has seen things no other man has and knows more than he can ever tell—and his story is an odyssey pulled out of a Hollywood movie.

If he had not become a cop, Alves believes he would have been the kind of person who spent his life investigating. "Before I was a cop, I was a street kid," he claims, spending his time on the streets of New Bedford and Fall River, learning the ins and outs of the harder side of the block. He often carried a gun and wore gang colors to intimidate people and earn respect. He began hanging out with criminals and listened closely to their stories. At school the next day, he would repeat them but claim credit for the crime. People feared him, but there was also an odd respect that came from it.

He became a part of the Freetown Auxiliary Police in 1971 by passing the qualifying test with the highest score and was promoted to a full time officer in 1973 by graduating first in his class. He was already gaining a reputation in the town for his police work, and the seeds of discrimination had already been planted. Some claimed he cheated on the test, and at the academy, because there was no way he could beat out white men. Alves, however, was a perfectionist and he knew being successful meant doing twice as much work as everyone else. In the early years many of the obstacles had to do with race, but in later years, the motives would change, and it is this change Alves believes should make the town uneasy.

A small town police officer is not the most glorious job in the world. Most of the day is spent settling domestic squabbles and supervising events, but Freetown's geography makes it attractive to criminals, especially those from the neighboring cities of New Bedford and Fall River. While on the job, he was the investigator for countless cases and was given a special award from George H. Bush for his work on a drug task force involving different cities and different local and federal agencies. He excelled in the field not because of his training from books, but because of his life as a thug. It had taught him how to cultivate relationships with people and how to use favors and give-and-take to gather information. More importantly, he now found his old friends the victims or suspects he was investigating. He knew more about the street because he had lived it, and the more time to spent investigating, the more he became someone criminals turned to for help.

Most police officers go their whole careers without every coming in contact with a murder investigation. In the late seventies and up through the nineties, Freetown became the stage for serial killers and Satanic murders, and Alan Alves was at the center of every major investigation. "In my time, I investigated eighteen murders," says Alves. "Eighteen. That number is ridiculous."

It was not the number that brought Alves to the forefront of the media and gained him national attention, but the nature of the crimes. It began with graffiti and animal remains. Everyone in town knew there were weird people in the forest at night. On one of his first nights with the force, Alves himself witnessed a ceremony deep within the state forest, but people were convinced it was the remains of a hippy culture that had all but died out across the country. The people dressing up, and starting fires in the forest was harmless and not worth the police's time.

The activity began to change. More dead animals were turning up and the graffiti was finding its way outside the forest. In some ways, the dead animals and large circles of rocks were becoming more obvious, but Alves saw more subtle things in the forest, a sign the cults had evolved and there was a more sophisticated element at work. Instead of the teenage graffiti, Alves began to find small upside down crosses in the forest going unnoticed. Often these crosses were carved into trees or looked like branches, but he began seeing more and more of them, often near surveyor markers. Following the trails left by these crosses, he would find sites of rituals.

The new cults were organized.

The more he investigated, the more he would hear whispers from old friends and informants. There were several cults active in the area. They mainly consisted of drug dealers, pimps and other criminals who used Satanism as a way to feel powerful and intimidate those under them. Most believed there was a way to use power to conjure Satan and have him grant them power, while others used it to thrill people and draw in lonely teenagers. Either way, the forest offered the perfect place for ceremonies, and the nature of their activity was much more criminal than the dabblers who had made the forest their home.

"I had to find out more," says Alves, who now makes his living as a hypnotherapist at the Southcoast Hypnosis Center in Fall River. "I didn't start out to be an expert, but I'd read up on things to understand what was going on. The more I read, the more people thought I was an authority. The more they thought I was an authority, the more I would have to read to know what I was talking about."

His research led him to join forces with authorities in Ohio and California. Together they formed the Cult Awareness Network, a group of law enforcement agents who dedicated themselves to gathering and sharing the information they were learning about the cults in their areas. Their work allowed the police to see how widespread the problem was throughout the country and also trained them what to look for.

The more Alves learned, the more he noticed the signs in his backyard. In addition to the crosses and animals, there were other things among the trees. He began to see small, voodoo dolls nailed to pieces of wood. He would also find discarded dolls and children's clothes in secluded areas.

The most disturbing discovery happened in November of 1988. A hunter in the woods came across a hidden fort inside the forest. It was covered over by a large tarp and leaves and was invisible unless it was approached from the right an-

The mausoleum where the head of Angie Littlefield
was found. *Courtesy of Big Operations Productions*

The secret den. *Courtesy of Big Operations Productions*

gle. When Alves investigated its contents, he knew the level of activity had shifted. Inside were small dolls with their eyes gouged out or burned. There were children's clothes scattered and stained and a small carved wooden chair. Among these artifacts were animal bones, ritualistic weapons and occult paraphernalia like dolls and witch's hats. Although none of the evidence could be linked to any specific crime, it served as notice of what was in the forest.

Alves was also being called outside his town to consult on cases other town were seeing. He investigated activity in nearby Dartmouth and Westport. The signs were all around. He was brought in on several cases on Cape Cod where child sex cases were being linked to ritual abuse. In every case, the facts were just below the surface, and despite evidence, almost every case died before going to court. Sometimes the local authorities refused to move ahead, citing a lack of evidence. Often, the District Attorneys would suppress the evidence, knowing the cult angle would open the door for reasonable doubt. Others were just dropped. Key people would start refusing his phone calls or an unexplained death of someone in charge of the investigation would stall the case.

It became clear to Alves there was a darker force at work. Suspects from one crime he was investigating began to implicate town officials as heads of cults. Although nothing could be used in court, a pattern was developing. Highly organized groups were using the smaller groups of pimps and drug dealers as their foot soldiers, often without them knowing, and using them to distract from their activities. Police and federal agencies found it difficult to bring many of these cults to justice. There was no way to infiltrate the groups, especially because so many of their initiations involved criminal activity and bizarre activities such as the drinking of blood, urine, and semen.

To Alves, these cults are like roaches. If you see one, there are more hidden in the walls. If you see evidence of a cult, you are not seeing the real cult. Members float from one fraction within the cult to another so people cannot detect everyone involved and where the leadership is.

He also began to see his personal life change. After being overlooked several times for promotion, he took the town to court. While he has suffered through discrimination since he had started the job, this was something new. He could take the burning crosses on his lawn, but not the hit to his livelihood. Over the next several years, he would fight for every promotion, winning every case. His image in the town was tainted, though. His credibility was in question and he was often viewed as a troublemaker. In 1997, he was brought up on phony sexual harassment charges, the details of which were leaked to the media during his hearing. There were also accusations he was leaking information to the media himself on cases he was investigating. Nothing much ever came of any of the charges against him, but they served to distract him.

Cases and evidence kept coming in. Besides several high profile cases involving the occult, such as the Satanic Murders and the Highway Killings, there was other evidence the cult was still active in the forest. In 1998, for example, there were two instances of animal mutilation in the woods. In April, a dozen calves where found mutilated. In October of the same year, the remains of a headless cow were found in the same spot. The dates of the killings coincided with Satanic holidays, but there were other signs it was the work of a more organized cult.

"Lack of blood. That's one of the big signs." According to Alves, the more advanced cults use the blood in different ways than the dabblers. Part of the ceremony is the gathering of the blood for use in other parts of the ritual, and their technique leaves little blood at the scene or in the animal. It also requires a level of patience not usually present with the smaller cults.

Much of the evidence of cult activity may never be found or connected. Alves and other law officials believe there are bodies hidden in the forest that will never be found and many of the random cases they have encountered over the years are linked but there is not enough evidence. Those who committed the crimes were too careful and too good at what they did. That is the most concrete proof they exist, but also the easiest to dismiss as being the product of overactive imaginations and conspiracy theorists.

Alves kept the big picture in his mind during his investigations, but tried to concentrate on the cases in front of him. Too many seemed to be linked. Each time he felt he was closing in on something big, something else would come up. Alves now wonders why. Given the favorable retirement he received, the large settlement in 1996, the additional $250,000 he received in 1999 for civil liberties violations, and the constant distraction of his attention, he firmly believes members of the larger cult wanted him away from his investigations and out of the picture.

"Without a doubt. They wanted my mind somewhere else. They were happy to see me go. They gave me everything I wanted when I retired. Everything."

He also believes the activity in the forest will never stop. Many of the smaller cults were flushed out of the area. The efforts of Steve Bates and others helped. There was also a small unofficial group formed that patrolled the forest. They brought baseball bats and other weapons with them and made it known that the cults were not welcome. It served its purpose at the time. People stopped using the forest for a while. The organized cult moved its activity to other towns, coming back to Freetown occasionally for ceremonies. The dabblers have returned, but even their activity seems more random.

A child's chair found in the secret Satanist den.
Courtesy of Big Operations Productions

CHAPTER 16

SATAN'S SHACK: THE CULT KILLINGS AND THEIR LEGACY

Sometimes a crime can be overlooked and easily forgotten. A body turns up and the facts seem like they are going to fall into place for the police. There is an element in southeastern Massachusetts steeped in a tradition of criminal activity, and when one of its own steps out of line, the resulting violence is disturbing but predictable. The newspapers might flare up if there is an angle, but the story fades after a while in favor of the next spark. The victim might leave behind a

The shack used by the Carl Drew/Robin Murphy cult. *Courtesy of Alan Alves*

family to mourn, but the world goes on turning and the names and details fade.

There should have been no reason for the state to remember the death of Doreen Ann Levesque. As one of thousands of prostitutes who have worked the streets of Fall River, her death might have not even warranted a second look from the people in her area. It was front page news on the day the body was discovered, but people should not know here name almost thirty years later. The discovery of her body, however, was the first chapter in one of the most sensational murder cases ever played out in a Massachusetts court room. The case is still being played out today through the appeals courts and still being debated in the court of public opinion throughout chat rooms on the internet. Everybody knows someone who was involved in the case and everyone has an opinion.

Outside of the area it is unlikely you know about Levesque or Carl Drew and Andy Maltais or Robin Murphy. People in Freetown remember the names like a roll call. They have appeared in the papers since 1979, and continue to be written and read about. People outside of the area cannot remember the names of the victims or the convicted, but they have heard of the Cult Killings.

Prostitutes sometime get killed. No life is worth more than another, but there is a lifestyle there that lends itself to violent behavior. When Levesque's body was found underneath the bleachers of the Diman Regional Vocational High School on October 13, 1979, the list of suspects was long but predictable. After she was identified as a prostitute, the investigation focused on old customers and her pimp, Carl Drew. While no motive was clear at the beginning, the reasons for the young girl's murder seemed part of the old story. Drew was a tough street kid who had built his reputation from violent encounters and running his ladies with a quick fist. Violence against prostitutes from their customers was nothing new. As Fall River evolved from a booming industrial town to a haven for drug addicts and street criminals, attacks became more frequent, usually going unreported. The case was not a major priority, but it soon became the center of a larger criminal ring developing out of the Freetown State Forest.

One of the first people to offer information about Levesque's killing was a man named Andy Maltais. He knew nothing himself, but was in contact with several other prostitutes who had information about the murder. Maltais was also a reformed Satanist and ran with a small cult located in Fall River. The focus of the investigation shifted to Maltais when his girlfriend, Barbara Raposa, also turned up dead a few months later. There were similarities in both of the murders. Both women had been bound previous to their death. Although there was proof of a knife wound on Levesque, both women had been killed by having their heads crushed with stones, an odd weapon of choice.

Maltais offered another link between the two murders. In the beginning of his relationship with the police, he had offered up a woman who had information about the first victim's killing. The woman, Karen Marsden, was also an employee of Carl Drew's and feared the man. According to the book, *Mortal Remains*, one of the most detailed accounts of the killing, Marsden often referred to the man as the Devil during interviews with police. She claimed he had killed Levesque and was going to kill her for speaking to the police. Although her career and drug addictions made her an unreliable witness, the police took her story seriously and encouraged her to give any information she could, especially when she also came forward with information about the Raposa murder. Over the course of several weeks, she opened up to the police and eventually told what little she could about the murder.

Another woman, Robin Murphy, was introduced to police by Maltais. Although she was a prostitute as well, she seemed to have a level of control over the other ladies she worked with, although it is unclear if this grew out of sexual relationships or her strong personality. According to Marsden, Murphy had driven her to the State Forest and threatened her life. She claimed to be involved in a cult who frequently used the woods and told the woman she would offer her and her son up to Satan. One thing was definite early on in her relationship with the police; Karen was sure she was going to die at the hands of Carl Drew.

Maltais was eventually arrested and convicted for the murder of his girlfriend. The major witness in the crime was Murphy who claimed he had killed her because she had cheated on him. He had taken her to a wooded area, had violent sex with her, and then killed her with a rock or a piece of cement. The confession sealed Maltais' fate, and thrust Murphy into the spotlight. Murphy also claimed to have helped kill Marsden with Drew to get her to remain silent on the Levesque murder.

Over the next year, cases were made and witnesses found. Drew was convicted of the murder of Karen Marsden, due (in large part) to witness testimony and inconstancies with his alibi. Maltais was convicted of killing his girlfriend, Barbara Raposa. Robin Murphy offered evidence against Drew during his trial and received a reduced sentence and immunity from any involvement in the other two cases. Drew remains in prison, Maltais died in prison in the late eighties, and Murphy was released from jail in 2004.

It would seem like an open and shut case. For some reason, three women were killed. All three ran in hard circles and engaged in prostitution and drugs. They had been murdered by pimps and lowlifes, and one had died because she had come forward against the group.

Things, however, were not that simple. Crucial to the crimes was the fact that those involved were either part of, or involved themselves with, a Satanic cult active in the area. The ritualistic aspects of the killings and the tales of conjuring the Devil and performing sexual acts against the dead bodies sparked the media interest. A dead hooker was one thing, but when that death became the calling card for occult killers, people became enthralled by the lives of this group of criminals.

To most, the picture was clear. Carl Drew, as the pimp, was the head of the cult. He believed in Satan and his power, but more likely used Satanic imagery as a way of keeping his girls in line. He was not the most religious man, but the power he received from keeping them scared became addictive. They were young girls with troubled childhoods and drug addictions. It was perfect soil for his ideas, and in turn, he used the rituals to keep them addicted and involve them in more serious crimes to keep them close. The cult focused on sex, drugs, and power. On the surface, its ideas were a combination of self-styled rituals and a twisting of ideas gathered from the Bible and the media.

They met in an apartment in Fall River, but most of their rituals were performed in the State Forest. There were stories of many people dying in the forest at the hands of the cult, but it is difficult to tell if this is true or whether it was part of the myth the group built around themselves. Working on information gathered by one witness, the police were able to find a makeshift shack in the woods where the group prepared for their ceremonies. It was the sight of orgies and preparations, although the murder of animals and other victims were always done a distance away from the house. Investigators found items consistent with cult activity, but nothing linked back to those on trial and nothing could be used in court.

The shack has become the subject of legend in the town. With so many details and so many true and fictitious stories going around, connections are made between unrelated subjects and names get confused. In some stories told about it, the shack is called the Ice House and is the sight of continued Satanic activity and paranormal disturbances. Those who hear the stories say it is the same shack, but others claim the Ice House to be another location in the Fall River section of the forest. If the structure still stands today, it is a testament to the fine craftsmanship of hookers and pimps, and remains out of the way enough to be seen by only a few.

The case still lingers today, and not just because Murphy is out free and Drew still fights for a new trial, proclaiming his innocence. Many people made their careers on the case. The convictions and the national exposure of the crimes made celebrities of those involved and signaled the turning point in law enforcement officials who worked it. When Henry Scammell released his book, *Mortal Remains,* in 1991, it made heroes of the participants, especially the Fall River Major Crimes Division working the case. Almost from the beginning, there were holes in the convictions.

While the details of the murders are murky at best, trying to sort through the ruble of the cases years later is like attacking a jungle with a butter knife. There have been accusations of witness tampering, police misconduct, and an ever-changing presentation of who did what to whom when. While most people remember the case through *Mortal Remain,* those who worked the case condemn the book and consider it an inaccurate account of the events.

Drew was convicted mainly through the testimony of his associates, most of whom were street people with addictions and agendas. More importantly, many were thought to be his accomplices in the crimes. Over the years, more has come out about the police's role in the convictions and the inconstancies of the details of the murders. Witnesses have recanted their testimonies, including Murphy, claiming they were bullied by the police and the district attorney into saying things against Drew. As late as 2004, those involved were taken to task about how they had gotten their information and what their witnesses had said on the stand. In that year, Drew filed for a new trial and his attorney brought forth witness after witness claiming that their words at his original trial were coerced. Old witnesses and police officers were brought before the court to retell their stories, but Drew was denied a new trial despite the negative pictures told about the investigation.

Most who were close to the case during the investigation doubt Carl Drew is guilty of the murder he is in jail for. Most agree, off the record, Robin Murphy was the actual leader of the cult and the driving force behind all three murders. According to sources, she was a master at controlling people and understanding what it took to set people against each other. It is also claimed her intelligence had been tested, and she had measured well into the genius range. Additionally, she recanted much of what she said as the years went on, late enough to ensure she would not be accused herself and yet early enough to shed doubt on the police's efforts throughout the investigations.

There were other things pointing to Murphy. During her confession to her involvement in the Raposa case, she was careful to separate herself from the murder and yet give details explaining away any forensic evidence the police found. They had fought in the back of the Maltais' car on the way to the murder scene, giving an excuse for any hair or skin found on the body. She also claimed to have bitten her during the exchange, a piece of evidence the police had kept hidden from the papers and one that would have helped identify the killer.

During Drew's trial in 2004, Carol Fletcher, originally one of the prime witnesses against him, claimed he was innocent. In her testimony, she also said she had witnessed a fight the night of the murder between Marsden and Murphy on the roof of a building and had left when Murphy took a knife out and approached the victim. Murphy also bragged about the crime the next day to her.

No evidence has officially been brought forward against Murphy, and she has served the time she was sentenced to. Until the day new evidence comes out and she is brought to trial, she is innocent of any further involvement in the crimes.

There might be a bigger picture being missed in the drama of these crimes. Others close to the case feel these murders were only a glimpse of the true scope of the violence of the group and that it may be connected to other occult crimes. While this might be easy to dismiss, there is some evidence and link to a large cult remaining active in the area.

Early on in the investigation, Maltais was implicated in a rash of other rapes and killings that mirrored what happened to the girls. Although no formal charges were ever filed and the investigations stalled, the residue of those accusations linger. Cults work where their victims can easily disappear and the names of the fallen are forgotten before they are known. The world of prostitutes is perfect for this. There is an endless stream of young, nameless girls whose families rarely file missing person reports. They fade into the background of the city, and when one is missing, another takes her place before she is missed. This was the world the cult knew as home. Many of the rumored dead are said to be buried in the State Forest, and several retired police officials back up this claim. The dead may be numbered in the dozens.

The true head of the cult might not be Robin Murphy or Carl Drew and might not have dissolved with their convictions. Where as Drew was said to be a believer who used Satan as a way to keep control over people, other cult members in the area point to a more organized cult who controlled the actions of the character in Fall River. They are thought to be an extension of another group still active today. As part of the revolving membership of this cult, some were able to help form the Drew/Murphy branch and influence their activities. They encouraged the murders and profited from the selling of sex and drugs from the group. When group was broken up, the members split up, shifting their focus to New Bedford, and their leadership to Westport, and then to Rhode Island.

It cannot be debated that cult activity sprang up in these areas over the next few years. A serial killer came to light in the late eighties and early nineties in that area, and the victims were also prostitutes who had a history of drug use. The rings implicated there were also said to be involved in heavy drug trafficking and child pornography. What can be debated is the connection between the two cults. Both used Satan as a way to control the weak and scare victims into silence. Could the same ideas spring up in two places at the same time or did the actions of the Fall River cult create a template for success to be followed in the coming years? Were the events in Fall River and Freetown just business or was there something more involved going on?

Most associated with the case have died or moved on, although there is nothing sinister about it. Officials have retired and find themselves the subject of speculation years later. It has been almost thirty years since Doreen Levesque was found, and time can be cruel to high-risk groups. Prostitution and drugs are still big business in Fall River, but the town has softened since then. The names and stories are still remembered by those in Freetown, however. The paper resurrects them every once in a while, but there is something else. It is not just the hidden shack or the mental markers where the crimes were said to happen. They can hear it in the trees of the forest, like something calling out to be recalled, and they are unsure if it is the voices of the dead or something evil in the woods calling the Devil back home.

CHAPTER 17

ANOTHER BOGEYMAN

Like a bad dream, James Kater will not go away. He sits in jail today, convicted three times of the same crime in the past twenty-five years, but is always ready to return to the public eye, like the villain in a bad slasher film. Each time his name is mentioned, there is a collective gasp followed by a look of contempt. He is the face of what is right and wrong with our criminal justice system, but the town has a hard time finding comfort in abstract debates about him. To the town he is the Boogeyman, the outsider who brought his perversion to their small town.

James Kater's journey to Freetown began in 1968, with the assault and attempted rape of a young girl from North Andover. Although he was convicted of the crime and sentenced to serve fifteen to twenty years in prison, he was released after only six and a half. The assault would have gone under the radar of most in law enforcement if it had not been for one odd detail. Kater had tied the girl to a tree and left her.

In the fall of 1978, two years after his release and while still on parole, another body was found in the Freetown State Forest. The young girl was found by two boys 100 yards off Copicut Road near a fork from the main path. She was found fully clothed, tied to an oak tree by her neck and body with her hands bound behind her back. To the police, the crimes were almost identical, although the second victim had died of exposure before she could escape. Almost immediately, evidence began to conflict. Original reports had said she had died of exposure, but the autopsy was inconclusive. Although her clogs were still on and there was no sign of dragging, she was believed to be tied to the tree after death. Eventually, a forensic specialist determined she had been tied to the tree alive and had died of postural asphyxiation because of the way she was bound. In other words, she was tied to the tree alive and lost consciousness, at which time she choked on the binding around her neck. The inconsistencies and mystery of the case were just beginning.

After consulting dental record and several personal items found nearby, including a copy of her report card found in her purse, the body was found to be fifteen-year-old Mary Lou Arruda, a sophomore from Raynham, who had gone missing in early September. The focus of the police narrowed on a man who had been a suspect for two months. Kater had been identified early on in the investigation and had been brought in to be interviewed by the police. A sketch drawn by a witness who had seen the teenager with a man in a 1976 Buick Opel had matched his general description. Her bike had been found in the woods near her house shortly after the car had been spotted leaving it. When they searched his car, they found several Boston Globe newspapers highlighting the kidnapping and unusual markings on his tires that matched ones found at the scene.

When the body was discovered, and the true nature of the young girl's final minutes disclosed, the details matched his earlier assault too closely to be ignored. In addition to the tying of the bodies, both girls had been abducted while walking their bikes near their homes. Kater was arrested at his home in late November of 1978 and charged with kidnapping and murder. The thirty-two year old was held without bail, while communities from Rhode Island to Boston began to scream for justice for Mary Lou. Justice would be a long time coming.

The trial became the heartbeat of the community. Who could have done such a thing to a sweet cheerleader with her life in front of her? Why had he brought her here into their community? From the beginning, the proceedings were anything but normal. His attorney attempted to get the trial moved to another venue, but the judge ruled the case was too far-reaching and the publicity already too great. After exhausting 110 prospective jurors, others had to be bused in from Fall River to empanel. Eventually six woman and ten men were chosen and the prosecution began its case.

For the next three months, the state of Massachusetts watched as the commonwealth brought forth evidence. They produced people who had seen his car in the area, one going so far as to say she had seen a bulky object under a blanket. An unsmoked cigarette found near Arruda's bike was matched to a pack found in Kater's car, the same brand he was seen smoking during his initial interview with the police about the case two months before the body was even found. The FBI produced an expert who testified the tire tracks were consistent with the ones found on the accused's car. Some of the most damaging evidence came from local store managers and employees. James Kater was getting married the day after the kidnapping, and he claimed to have been driving all around doing errands at the time she was taken.

No significant eye witness could be found to back up his story.

Kater was found guilty of murder and kidnapping in the first degree. This would usually put the case to rest, but crime in Freetown has a habit of coming back around. A few years later, the conviction was overturned, as was another conviction in 1985. In both circumstances, crucial evidence was retrieved by a witness under hypnosis and deemed inadmissible in a court of law. While all the evidence pointed to Kater, he was on the verge of getting out. In 1992, with the accused spending every moment of his life behind bars since his arrest in 1978, Kater's latest trial ended in a mistrial. The community was outraged. After spending so much time grieving and trying to put the case behind them, the man who had haunted their lives seemed protected from judgment.

The murderer could go free.

The fourth trial, in late 1996, proved to be different. Kater's first victim, the survivor of the 1968 attack, was allowed to take the stand. The previous crime was allowed in during this trial because it was determined that it did not ask the jury to consider whether a man who committed one crime could commit another, but rather it offered a link between two crime scenes that were almost identical. This was the final link for the jury. Physical evidence and coincidence were one thing, but a living person, retelling her ordeal, finally did Kater in. On December 23, 1996, he was finally convicted.

There is another aspect of the crime which leaked out over the years. Alan Alves had been the first official on the site and had taken his own set of crime scene photos, including several of a ten-foot-high cross with pink cloth on it in the general area of the body. As details of Satanic activity came out over the next two decades, James Kater began providing another possible explanation for the Arruda murder: cults had killed the young girl. The alternate theory held some weight. There seemed to be cults active in the area, and there was proof some of these cults were capable of murder.

Alves disagrees with the idea. While there have been cult-related crimes in the area, and there has been a tentative link between the Highway Killer and a cult activity, the crime does not fit the usual profile. In the past, the victims have been members of the cult or people just on the outside of the circle. They have generally been prostitutes and drug addicts, not young girls with no criminal connection. Also, the cross at the crime was determined to predate the abduction and have no relevance to the crime. Lastly, the other victims had been local, and had not been taken from a town twenty minutes away.

"It's grasping at straws," Alves still believes today. The argument to him is a good one, but it does not hold water under the light of scrutiny. There might still be a link between the cults and the murderer. Part of the judgment of premeditation on Kater's part was he that had thought about the crime as he drove out to Freetown. It was not a crime of passion, but had been planned as he made his way down Route 24 to the State Forest. Why had he been drawn to this place in particular, especially a section of the forest that has seen multiple rapes and paranormal activity? Could it be he was drawn in by the same force felt by the cults who use the forest? Perhaps, like many things in Freetown, the energy offered him a safe haven for what he intended to do and called to him. The energy did not make him evil; it only created a field for him to play on.

If it sounds unreasonable, examine James Kater's first crime. He kidnapped the girl from North Andover and took her twenty minutes away. It might not be coincidence that a cult was discovered in that same area only a few years later. Although nothing came from the accusations and investigations into the suspected cult, it implicated several high-ranking officials and law enforcement officers in Essex County, Massachusetts. It finally died before full disclosure. Kater is most likely not a member of any cult himself, but he seems to have a knack for finding them.

Time cannot contain the memories of those who remember the early days of the abduction and trial. It still lives with them as part of their collective memory, a shared moment that never ends. Most believe he will never get out, but there is a flash where that conviction falters. James Kater has nine lives. They have seen him step out of the limelight only to return too many times. They have shut the book once too often and found another chapter they had not read yet. Two communities, once brought together to grieve and ask why, still have something in common. No matter how many times they tell themselves he will never see the light of day, he still walks the forest.

CHAPTER 18

THE HIGHWAY KILLER

In November of 2005, a female body was found on the side of the road near the intersection of Routes 88 and 195 in Westport. Dumped bodies are nothing new in that section of Massachusetts, but the message board of the local paper recorded an odd hysteria hitting the community almost immediately. A serial killer had struck again, stretching his hand from the early nineties into the new millennium to claim another victim. Although the case had been cold for almost a decade, people remembered the fear of the years when a murderer drove the streets, prowling for victims and alluding police. They were sure, as they had been so many times in the past few years, the Highway Killer had come out of hiding again.

The hysteria was commonplace by the time it hit the internet in 2005. Of all the criminals in the history of southeastern Massachusetts, none evoke fear like the one who got away. Whenever someone goes missing or a bone is found in the woods, people turn to him again, convinced he has awoken from his sleep. To many in the District Attorneys office, the case is closed, but it will never be over for the people who lived through the events or for the family members who have never seen justice for their lost loved ones. Everyone has a theory on who the killer is, and that may be how they deal with the uncertainty of it.

To many, the Highway Killer is alive, not just in their memories, but still walking the street, adding to his count.

The official total, according to sources, is eleven women, but most will tell you, off the record, the count may be as high as twenty. The first woman was found off Route 140 in Freetown in the summer of 1988. She was later identified as Debra Medeiros, a prostitute and drug dealer who worked out of New Bedford. Her body was found with her underwear discarded and her brassiere wrapped around her neck, which was the believed to be the method of death. The body was decomposing and had been dumped there some months before. Alan Alves was the first investigator on the scene and an associate of Medeiros.

Over the next few months, more woman began to disappear and bodies began to be found on the sides of highways in Bristol County. The murders themselves were similar, but a stronger connection was being made between the victims which forced the police to take a closer look at their missing persons roster. All were prostitutes with drug habits who were known to work in New Bedford, as were many of the missing women being reported by friends and family. Their physical descriptions were similar, although not striking or unique given the demographics of the area.

Hookers did not seem to be the top priority of the police, however, and the case was slow to develop, the first break the killer would receive from authorities. It was not until November of 1988, with the discovery of a third victim, that police began to see the patterns of a serial killer. It was also the point at which Alves noticed another similarity not generally written about when reviewing the case. Close to the scene of the first victim was a makeshift cross. Alves had trained himself to look for such things in his investigations because so much of the crime in Freetown was linked to cults. He also found crosses at the third murder scene, and it became clear to him there might be a link between the killings and any number of active cults in the area. According to Alves, a cross or alter was found in the area of every victim.

Consider the dates of the abductions and murders of the women. Most coincided with important dates on the Satanic Calendar. More importantly, 1988 marked an increase in cult activity throughout the state. Slaughtered animals were being found across the eastern counties of Massachusetts and police were observing more and more ceremonies and graffiti of an occult nature. The rise in exposure mirrored what was being seen throughout the United States that year. As the case played out, Alves found more evidence that the occult was connected to the murders, but he was laughed at and eventually dismissed from the taskforce.

The police widened their search, asking people for information and bringing in psychics and dogs to search for more bodies. Despite the fervor the case still inspires, many people did not pay attention to what was going on. Instead, many saw it as something happening to people they did not know, maybe even people who deserved it, and far away from their daily lives. This was the next element the killer was able to use to his advantage. If it had not been for several vocal family members and news reporters paying attention to the case, it might have slipped out of people's minds.

More bodies were found throughout the winter. While the number of dead was allowing the police to make connections between the killings, it was also helping to hide the killer's identity. The bodies were found in different towns, making it harder for police to share information and come up with a consistent plan of action. Each cop knew their territory, and many had egos interfering with the investigation.

What made solving the murders harder was the involvement of the District Attorney, Ron Pina, and the involvement of the state police as the arm of his office. The state police had an excellent handle on the big picture of the case, or at least the big picture Pina pointed them to. The trouble was, they were not effective investigators on a local level. They were not trained well enough and lacked a general knowledge of the area. They had almost no contacts within the communities and were often replaced by the DA. The victims and suspects in the case, along with the witnesses and the people with the vital information, were on the other side of the law, slow to trust and share.

Pina used the courts to further the investigation. He convened a grand jury to compel people to come forth with information. This proved to be the killer's ultimate ally. Without immunity and without a guarantee of protection, witnesses refused to testify to what they knew. The circle of junkies and prostitutes who could have broken the case open, and any information they had was cut off. "No one wanted to talk," says Alves. "The grand jury drove the information back underground."

Despite five major suspects in the crime, Pina's main focus was one, Kenneth Ponte. Ponte was an attorney with a sketchy background who was implicated in a major drug, pornography, and prostitution ring in the area. It is also believed by some that Pina had a personal grudge against him, and that is why it was pursued with some vigor. Several authorities close to the case say this focus allowed vital information to be dismissed after a taskforce was formed to work on the case full time. Despite the whispers about impropriety, Pina can only really be held accountable for his lack of vision in the case.

Ponte was eventually cleared of the crime, as was another major suspect, Tony Grazia. If Ponte seemed like a ringleader, capable of organizing crime in New Bedford, Tony seemed like the foot soldier. A large man with a deformed arm, he was known as a sweetheart by those close to him and as a devil by the prostitutes he picked up and beat. Even after becoming close with a beautiful young girl from the area, he still trolled the streets and became known as a bad customer. He was seen near some of the victims close to their disappearance and was well known to the police. He was capable of vicious assaults, so murder was not farfetched.

Tony seemed to mark a turning point in the case. It is hard to simplify something as complex as the circus that formed around the Highway Killer. As Pina and the police continued to come up dry in their investigation, people began to call for their heads. They were painted as bumbling fools, especially by people who had something to gain from making them look bad.

In July of 1991, Tony killed himself. Many figured the case had been solved. The police were closing in on him and the guilt made him take his own life. A lull in victims following his death has solidified the idea in many people's minds, but those close to the case feel Tony is innocent. They feel his relationship with a young lady led to his suicide. After she had left him, he had done anything he could to get her back, but on the day before he took his life, he found out she was pregnant with another man's baby.

The case is all but dead now. The families continue to speak out and the people bring it up whenever another body is found, but no one is doing much to solve the crimes. After Tony's death and continued clearings of suspects, the case lost momentum. When Pina lost his bid for reelection, the case stalled completely. There seems to be several theories out there, and at times the accusations overlap.

Many close to the case feel the killer is still out there. Several have come out and connected other killings in Massachusetts to the Highway Killer. One theory is he moved out of state, and similar murders after 1991, in parts of New England and other states are offered as evidence. Some feel the killer is in jail, caught on another charge and waiting to serve out his time so he can get out and continue his life's work

After his own retirement, Alan Alves' theories on the killer gained more attention. Although he has several, the occult angle is echoed by others who worked the case. The most dominant theory is a larger, more organized cult, the same one responsible for the formation of the Drew/Murphy cult, had a hand in the New Bedford crimes. Both involved prostitution and drugs and some of the periphery cast of that circle moved on and worked out of a bar in New Bedford. These murders are part of the bigger picture, the work of a group who give people a peak behind the curtain, only to cast us out when the level of dread reaches an appropriate pitch. About every decade or so, some case comes up that reveals their actions, but the left hand does not always know what the right hand is doing, and we only rarely glimpse them.

A drug and pornography ring suspected to be connected with the same club fits in with the established actions of such a cult. Police suspected the people were connected to the killings somehow, but they are still reluctant to make the leap to Satanic cults being the driving force behind the murders.

The killer can still bring the headlines and ruin careers. He was a major focus of the campaign of Sam Sutter in his bid to become the district attorney in 2006. He claimed the incumbent, Paul F. Walsh who had won the job from Pina, had done little to solve the case. He also pointed to other unsolved murders as potentially being connected and claimed it would be a top priority if he was elected. He won in what many consider a major upset, and in the Spring of 2007 he officially reopened the case, again focusing on Ponte.

CHAPTER 19

CONCLUSIONS ON CRIME, CONSPIRACIES, AND THINGS THAT GO BUMP IN THE NIGHT

Look away and the details change. Look too close and you miss the big picture. Look at the big picture and the small subtleties get overlooked. A conspiracy, almost by definition, cannot be proven, and if there is a grand plan to the cult activity in southeastern Massachusetts, this is the battlefield the puppeteers would choose. There is enough evidence to prove cults have used the forest and the surrounding towns for their crimes, but the proof of a larger conspiracy slips though the fingers, just when the image becomes clear. It is a double-edged sword. Is it human nature causing the failures of the police and attorneys connected with these cases, or are their actions being manipulated? Does the location of the forest attract the criminal element or does the energy of some unseen force or the controllers of chaos invite them in by posting a flashing neon sign just above the sign welcoming you to Freetown.

Many of these killings are connected, but the geography causes problems that help to bury the investigations. Similar crimes in different towns and different counties cause too many cooks to come to the pot. That kind of confusion is the goal of Satanic cults. The very nature of the crimes suggest a level of planning designed to remind people that evil exists and to intimidate and yet, at the same time, always keep the larger aim out of reach. How high does the contamination go and why do they choose Freetown? Are they drawn in by some energy they find there?

We can only speculate. Take the Kater case. According to several published accounts, there were two holes in her temple that might have indicated she had been shot. These were explained away as worm holes by the medical examiner. Other aspects of the crime were hidden from the courts, and Kater became a simple case of an escalating sexual crime. During the first abduction the victim was held under the water, but she fought back and Kater tied her up and left her out there. Why is it then a leap to assume the tying up of

A marker at the reservation. The colors and design mirrors a symbol common in Satanism.

the body had aroused him and encouraged him to repeat the action, and having learned from his earlier conviction, he shot and killed the victim so she could not identify him? Why were prosecutors so set on having identical crimes when a jury could have made that connection?

A few days after he was picked up and charged with the murder, Kater's house was broken into and a fire set. Police had already checked the house for evidence, but could there have been evidence linking him to cult activity destroyed. At the time, the fire was played off as a vigilante attack, but a connection might have been severed in the blaze. Both of his crimes were committed in areas of high cult activity, but his silence on the matter has reinforced the idea he acted alone and with no higher orders from above.

In the Cult Killings, there has been much made of the Satanic beliefs of the major players, but little evidence was admitted having to do with the cult, other than the power structure it created. No one above the convicted was implicated and the cult angle was downplayed from the start. The murder that sparked the entire affair was never brought to trial and the digging stopped. The abuse of civil liberties of the District Attorney and the police may be a case of overzealous prosecution, but might also be evidence of getting the case out of the media before the real masterminds could be flushed out. Keep in mind, many of the members never served time and spread themselves out around the country after the trials were over.

In 2006, Carl Drew leaked out a revised statement from jail entitled "Blind Justice." Drew is a criminal and his words should be taken with a grain of salt, but members of the legal and law enforcement communities agree with what he says. He quotes Paul Carey, one of the lead investigators on the case, a major character in *Mortal Remains*. Carey preaches Drew's innocence and condemns Murphy as the leader. Was it only political pressure that forced the District Attorney into making the deal with her? Why was she allowed to be released after telling conflicting stories throughout her incarceration?

The Highway Killer still walks the streets. It might have been luck or careful planning that secured him, confusing different agencies and an entire taskforce into searching for a ghost. Again and again, facts of the case pointed to something bigger, and the theories, one by one, lost steam. Why were Alan Alves' theories dismissed and his career put on hold so he could defend his character time and again?

How many bodies are buried in the woods? According to law enforcement, the undiscovered may be as high as twenty or thirty. Those estimates are calculated in modern terms. What about the soldiers and Native Americans who might have died there during King Philip's War or the Wampanoags who died there before that conflict ever took place? There are also the reports of large numbers of slaves killed when slavery was outlawed in Massachusetts. How many souls will never be laid to rest?

Why is this small town the scene for so much tragedy, and why are there so many reports of the unexplained? Is any of this connected? Is Freetown cursed?

Evidence is based on fact, but what happens when your facts are shadows? If you diagram the stories out on a board, like they do on police dramas on television, the connection exists. Coincidence cannot be played out over decades or centuries. The pattern tells the story, but the suspect creeps away. There is no who or why, only evidence *something* exists.

During a recent radio interview, my ideas about the Cursed County and Freetown as the heart of negative energy in Massachusetts was laughed off. The host claimed he could walk down the street and show me half a dozen buildings that were haunted. His town, he said, had just as many ghosts as Freetown, and his were better because they had great stories attached to them.

There is the difference. The ghost of a man shot during a game of poker is not alive in Freetown. A known sunken ship does not appear in the water and fade away. Ghosts are big business, but there is no tavern in the town advertising a phantom moving the chairs at night. There is no back story to most of the specters in the forest, but rather something unexplained playing itself out for people in the present. There is a great New England myth about a woman, wrongfully accused of witchcraft, who places a curse on the town. To this day, nothing will grow on her grave. The curse in Freetown is real, but things continue to grow there. The redwoods planted decades ago grow straight, like great telephone poles in the forest. The legends grow too, and with each generation there are more stories to whisper once you have left the woods and you are safe in your home. During the day, the Freetown State Forest is a great place to take the family, but when the sun goes down, the stories linger, staining the landscape like burnt-out cars or graffiti on rocks.

BIBLIOGRAPHY

Blood, Linda. *The New Satanists*. New York, NY: Warner Books, 1994.

Brunvard, Jan Harold. *The Encyclopedia of Urban Legends*. Santa Barbara, CA: ABC-CLIO, Inc., 2001.

Cadieux, Aaron. *Inside the Bridgewater Triangle*. Big Operations Productions, 2003. Film

Citro, Joseph. *Strange Passing: True Tales of New England Hauntings and Horrors*. New York, NY: Houghton Mifflin Company, 1996.

Citro, Joseph. *Curious New England: The Unconventional Traveler's Guide to Eccentric Destinations*. Lebanon, NH: University Press of New England, 2003.

Coleman, Loren. *Mysterious America*. Boston, MA: Faber and Faber, 1983.

"Colonial Period (1675-1775)." Friends of Historic Preservation. Retrieved 10 March 2006. http://www.assonetriver.com/preservation/dist_period.asp?P=COL.

"Contact Period (1500-1620)." Friends of Historic Preservation. Retrieved 10 March 2006. http://www.assonetriver.com/preservation/dist_period.?P=CP.

"Dighton Rock State Park." MassParks. Retrieved 31 October 2003. http://www.state.ma.us/dem/parks/digr.htm.

"Docket No. SJC-07867." "Findlaw: For Legal Professionals." Retrieved 18 January 2007. http://caselaw.lp.findlaw.com/scripts/getcase. pl?court=ma&vol=sjcslip/7967&invol=1.

Drake, James. *King Philip's War: Civil War in New England 1675-1676.* Amherst, MA: The University of Massachusetts Press, 1990.

"Early Industrial Period (1830-1870)." Friends of Historic Preservation. Retrieved 10 March 2006. http://www. assonetriver.com/preservation/dist_period.asp?P=EI.

"Early Modern Period (1915-1949)." Friends of Historic Preservation. Retrieved 10 March 2006. http://www.assonetriver.com/preservation/dist_period.asp?P=EM.

"First Settlement Period (1620-1675)." Friends of Historic Preservation. Retrieved 10 March 2006. http://www. assonetriver.com/preservation/dist_period.asp?P=FSP.

"Freetown-Fall River State Forest." MassParks. Retrived 31 October 2003. http://www.state.ma.us/dem/parks/ free.htm.

"Freetown-Fall River State Forest." Wikipedia, the free Encyclopedia. Retrieved 4 February 2006. http:// en.wikipedia.org/wiki/Freetown-Fall_River_State_Forest.

"Freetown, Massachusetts." Wikipedia, the free Encyclopedia. Retrieved 10 March 2006. http://en.wikipedia. org/wiki/Freetown_Massachusets.

"Freetown Town Information." SouthCoast Today. Retrieved 7 August 2003. http://www.southcoasttoday. com/2002/freeinfo.htm.

Fritz, Jean. *The Good Giants and the Bad Pukwudgies.* New York, NY: G.P. Putnam's Sons, 1983.

Greer, John Michael. *The New Encyclopedia of the Occult.* St. Paul, MN: Llewellyn Publications, 2003.

John Estrella, "But Even Now, Many Fear Murderer Might Walk Free," *Standard-Times,* 25 December 1996.

"Late Industrial Period (1870-1915)." Friends of Historic Preservation. Retrieved 10 March 2006. http://www.assonetriver.com/preservation/dist_period.asp?P=LI.

LaVey, Anton Szandor. *The Satanic Bible.* New York, NY: Avon Books, 1969.

Mack, Carol K. and Dinah Mack. *A Field Guide to Demons: Fairies, Fallen Angels and Other Subversive Spirits.* New York, NY: Owl Books, 1998.

"The Mad Trucker of Copicutt Road." New England Legends. Retrieved 24 August 2006. http://www.free-webs.com/newenglandlegends/madtruckfreetown.htm.

Marcus, Jon. *Unknown New England: Landmarks, Museums, and Historical Sites You Never Knew Existed.* Bloomington, IN: 1st Books, 2003.

Maureen Boyle, "Kater's Endless Appeals Raise Judicial Questions," *Standard-Times,* 26 January 1997.

"Question of Evidence: Kater's Attorneys Accuse Prosecution of Misconduct," *The Herald News,* 16 October 1996.

Reynard, Elizabeth. The *Narrow Land: Folk Chronicles of Old Cape Cod*. Chatham, MA: The Chatham Historical Society, Inc., 1978.

Ric Oliveira, "Da: Arruda Case is Closed," *Standard-Times*, 25 December 1996.

Robinson, Charles Turek. *The New England Ghost Files An Authentic Compendium of Frightening Phantoms*. North Attleboro, MA: Covered Bridge Press, 1994.

Robinson, Charles Turek. *True New England Mysteries, Ghosts, Crimes, and Oddities*. North Attleboro, MA: Covered Bridge Press, 1994.

"Secrets of a Serial Killer." WHDH-TV Boston. Retrieved 25 May 2005. http:www.whdh.com/features/articles/specialreport/A238/.

Scammel, Henry. *Mortal Remains: Bizarre Serial Killings Stun a Small New England Town*. New York, NY: Haper-Paperbacks, 1991.

Smith, Carlton. *Killing Season: The Unsolved Case of New England's Deadliest Serial Killer*. New York, NY: Onyx Books, 1994.

Venables, Robert W. *American Indian History: Five Centuries of Conflict and Coexistence*. Sante Fe, NM: Clear Light Publishing, 2004.

Zachary R. Dowdy, "Defense Cites Cult Ties in '78 Slaying," *The Boston Globe*, 16 October 1996.

Zachary R. Dowdy, "Judge Clears the Way for a Fourth Trial in Girl's 1978 Killing," *The Boston Globe*, 17 October 1996.